Published by:
Airlife Publishing Ltd
101 Longden Road
Shrewsbury SY3 9EB
England
Telephone: 01743 235651
Fax: 01743 232944

Produced by Aerospace Publishing Ltd and
published jointly with Airlife Publishing Ltd

Copyright © 1996 Aerospace Publishing Ltd

Author:
  Chris Bishop
Sub-Editor:
  Trisha Palmer
Design:
  Vanessa Stoddart
  Hilary Speller

First published 1996

ISBN 1-85310-539-2

Printed in Singapore

THE VITAL GUIDE TO

COMBAT GUNS

AND INFANTRY WEAPONS

EDITOR: CHRIS BISHOP

Airlife

England

Picture acknowledgements

8: Steyr-Mannlicher/Fabrique National. **9:** (top) Fabrique National. **13:** (bottom) Walther. **14:** (top and middle) Heckler & Koch. **16:** (top) Beretta. **17:** Star Bonifacio Echeverria. **18:** (top) Associated Press /(middle) SIG. **19:** SIG. **20:** (bottom) US Army. **21:** (top) Colt. **22:** US Air Force/Sturm, Ruger. **26:** (top) Australian DoD. **27:** (bottom left and right) Steyr-Mannlicher. **28:** (top) Associated Press. **29:** (top) Tampeeren. **30:** Associated Press/Walther. **31:** (top) Press Association. **32:** (top) Herman Potgieter. **33:** Beretta. **34:** (bottom) SITES. **36:** (top) UK MoD. **37:** (top) US Army. **41:** Steyr-Mannlicher (both) **42:** (top) Royal Netherlands Marines. **43:** (top) Fabrique National. **45:** (top) ECPA. **46:** Norwegian MoD (both). **49:** (top) Beretta. **50:** Chartered Firearms Industries/ Armscor. **51:** (bottom) CETME. **52:** (top) SIG. **53:** (top) Press Association. **54:** (bottom) US National Archives. **55:** US DoD (both). **56:** (top) US Army. **57:** (top) US DoD. **59:** (bottom) Associated Press. **62:** Beretta. **63:** Steyr-Mannlicher/ECPA. **64:** (top) Heckler & Koch. **65:** IMI/Beretta. **68:** US DoD (all). **69:** US DoD (all). **70:** (bottom) Chris Bishop. **73:** Fabrique National (both). **74:** US DoD/Fabrique National. **75:** (bottom) Yves Debay. **77:** Heckler & Koch/SIG. **78:** (top) Herman Potgieter. **80:** (top) US DoD. **81:** (top) US Army. **83:** (top) US DoD. **85:** (bottom) Franchi. **86:** Beretta/Armsel. **87:** US Marine Corps/Pancor. **88:** Smith & Wesson/Olin Industries. **90:** (top) Steyr-Mannlicher. **91:** (top) Vainenninmetalli. **92:** (bottom right) Royal Marines Museum. **95:** Heckler & Koch/Chartered Firearms Industries. **96:** (top) US DoD. **97:** (top) US Army. **99:** British Aerospace. **101:** US Army. **104:** Euromissile (both). **105:** Euromissile (both). **106:** Aéro-spatiale/IMI. **108:** AB Bofors/ NobelTech. **110:** Armscor/US Army. **111:** McDonnell Douglas/US DoD. **112:** Hughes (both) **113:** (bottom) Associated Press. **115:** (top) US DoD. **116:** Short Brothers. **117:** Matra/NobelTech. **118:** Short Brothers (both). **119:** Short Brothers (three). **120:** General Dynamics/US DoD. **121:** Finnish MoD/US DoD.

All other pictures: Aerospace Publishing Ltd

CONTENTS

PISTOLS

AUSTRIA
Glock self-loading pistol

IN 1983 AN AUSTRIAN COMPANY that made entrenching tools was the surprise winner of the Austrian army's pistol trials. The innovative **Glock 17** pistol has gone on to become a market leader in a little more than a decade.

Press reports that it was X-ray proof and thus a terrorist's dream were nonsense; it has a steel barrel and slide. Even so, with just 33 parts it is astonishingly simple to maintain, and its pioneering use of a high-impact polymer frame raised a few eyebrows. Although it uses a conventional tilt-locking system, the Glock has a unique self-cocking mechanism that incorporates three internal safeties. There is no external safety catch. The trigger safety, firing-pin lock and trigger bar safeties keep the weapon safe until the trigger is pulled.

The Glock was well marketed, and in addition to military sales captured an increasing share of the

Developed by a company with no prior firearms-manufacturing experience, the tough, reliable Glock pistol has achieved considerable success.

civilian and police markets. Other variants include the 10-mm **Glock 20**, the .45-calibre **Glock 21** and the **Glock 23**, which fires the increasingly popular .40-inch S&W cartridge. Glock moved so fast that it came close to beating Smith & Wesson at producing a gun to fire the Massachusetts company's own cartridge. The Model 23 is externally similar to the other Glock pistols and is well placed to collect large orders from US law enforcement agencies. The .40 S&W cartridge has taken the police market by storm, and the Glock's simplicity of operation is popular with departments changing from revolvers to automatics.

The Glock was one of the first pistols to make extensive use of composites and plastics in its construction, a practice which has become much more common since the weapon's introduction.

SPECIFICATION
Name: Glock 17
Type: self-loading pistol
Calibre: 9-mm x 19 Parabellum
Weight: (empty) 656 g
Dimensions: length 185 mm; barrel length 114 mm
Muzzle velocity: 360 metres per second
Magazine capacity: 17-round box
Users: police and security forces in more than 42 countries

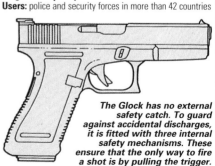

The Glock has no external safety catch. To guard against accidental discharges, it is fitted with three internal safety mechanisms. These ensure that the only way to fire a shot is by pulling the trigger.

AUSTRIA
GB self-loading pistol

The Steyr GB is a large, accurate pistol. Its high-capacity magazine holds 18 rounds.

THE LARGE STEYR-DAIMLER-PUCH group of Austria incorporates the old Österreichische Waffenfabrik of Steyr. The company has a long tradition of pistol manufacture, and in the shape of various Mannlicher and Steyr designs was responsible for some of the earliest practical self-loading pistols. Steyr continued its tradition of innovative design with the **Pi 18** pistol, which when suitably modified went into production as the **GB.**

In many ways, the GB is an unusual design. When first introduced the 18-round magazine capacity seemed enormous, almost double the load of many of its rivals and three times the capacity of a service revolver. It is a fairly bulky weapon, not really designed for concealed carry. Many other large-capacity pistols have reached the market since then.

The most unusual feature of the GB is its working parts. Most pistols are simply blowback-operated, but the big Austrian handgun taps off a small amount of propellant gas to keep the weapon locked until the bullet is clear of the barrel and the breech pressure has dropped. As a side benefit, the gas-delayed blowback action allied to the GB's relatively large size absorbs recoil excellently, and the gun is capable of great accuracy. The GB is issued with the now-common three-dot sighting system for rapid sight alignment, giving a good clear picture.

SPECIFICATION
Name: GB
Type: self-loading pistol
Calibre: 9-mm x 19 Parabellum
Weight: (empty) 845 g
Dimensions: length 216 mm; barrel length 136 mm
Muzzle velocity: (depending on cartridge used) 360-420 metres per second
Magazine capacity: 18-round box
Users: some European police forces

BELGIUM
BDA 9 self-loading pistol

Fabrique National's double-action pistols take the Browning High Power design, which for all its undoubted success has been around for more than half a century and is showing its age, and add safety features which bring it up to date.

SPECIFICATION
Name: BDA 9
Type: self-loading pistol
Calibre: 9-mm x 19 Parabellum
Weight: (empty) 905 g
Dimensions: length 200 mm; barrel length 118 mm
Muzzle velocity: 350 metres per second
Magazine capacity: 14-round box
Users: Belgian police and some security forces

DERIVED BY FABRIQUE NATIONAL from the famous FN Browning High Power, the **BDA 9** retains many of the characteristics that have made the older pistol a best-seller for half a century. It uses the same short-recoil system with a cam beneath the breech to disengage the trigger, but with a double-action trigger.

As with most modern pistols, the BDA is designed to be fired left- or right-handed. It has a decocking lever on both sides of the slide and a magazine release catch that can be reversed in seconds. The trigger guard has been reshaped to allow for a two-handed combat grip.

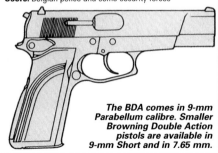

The BDA comes in 9-mm Parabellum calibre. Smaller Browning Double Action pistols are available in 9-mm Short and in 7.65 mm.

Browning High Power self-loading pistol

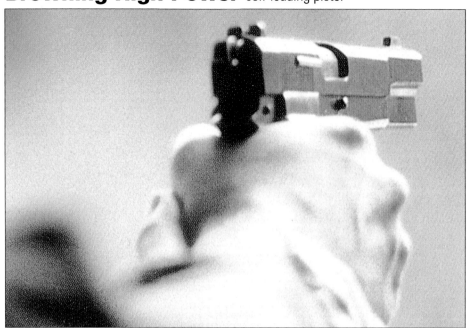

THE **BROWNING MODEL 35 High Power** was designed in the 1920s by the great John M. Browning. Produced by Fabrique National in Belgium as the **GP** or **Grande Puissance**, it is one of the most successful military pistols of all time.

The Browning may be old, but it remains in widespread use. It was the first of the modern large-capacity pistols, and its 13-round magazine, allied to a simple design and rugged toughness testified to by a 50-year combat record, all count in its favour.

The Browning's action was adapted from that used on the Colt Model 1911, but improved and simplified, which enhanced both reliability and ease of maintenance.

Used by British and Commonwealth forces since World War II, it is still in service, although in 1990 the British Army ordered a limited purchase of SIG-Sauer

One of the great firearms designs, the reliable Browning High Power was the first of the modern high-capacity pistols. Introduced as the Grande Puissance in the 1930s, its 13-round capacity has been tested to the full in innumerable conflicts since then.

pistols for Special Forces use. Fabrique National has developed several modernised versions of the High Power, but none has caught on like the original.

SPECIFICATION

Name: Browning High Power
Type: self-loading pistol
Calibre: 9-mm x 19 Parabellum
Weight: (empty) 882 g
Dimensions: length 200 mm; barrel length 136 mm
Muzzle velocity: 350 metres per second
Magazine capacity: 13-round box
Users: most NATO armies, over 50 countries worldwide

The Browning Compact was developed from the High Power as a pocket pistol capable of firing full-power 9-mm rounds.

The High Power's grip contains the 13-round magazine, which was almost double the capacity of its contemporaries.

9

CZECH REPUBLIC
CZ75 self-loading pistol

The CZ75 is an excellent security weapon, easily the match of any of the high-tech products of Western gun manufacturers.

shooters in Europe and the USA.

Unfortunately the design was not patented in the West, and key features have been copied by other manufacturers. The Czechs have fought back with the **CZ85**, which has ambidextrous controls and a better finish, and the exceptionally accurate AT-2000 version licence-built in Switzerland by Sphinx has achieved considerable export success.

SPECIFICATION
Name: CZ75
Type: self-loading pistol
Calibre: 9-mm x 19 Parabellum
Weight: (empty) 980 g
Dimensions: length 203 mm; barrel length 120 mm
Muzzle velocity: 360 metres per second
Magazine capacity: 15-round box
Users: Czech and Slovak forces

Using a modified Colt/ Browning operating system, the CZ75 has excellent balance and pointing qualities.

PRODUCED IN CZECHOSLOVAKIA before the collapse of the Warsaw Pact, the excellent **Model 75** or **CZ75** 9-mm pistol continues a tradition of quality Czech small-arms design. It is a sound combat pistol with a large-capacity double-row magazine and a surprisingly smooth double action, which has became very popular with sports

---

FRANCE
PA 15 self-loading pistol

The PA15, often known as the MAB after its manufacturer, has a complex operating system.

The PA 15 has a bulky grip, needed to house the 15 Parabellum rounds it holds in its magazine. It has a relatively complex delayed blowback semi-automatic locking system, resulting from the fact the fact that the PA15 was originally designed to fire less powerful rounds than the 9-mm Parabellum. No longer manufactured in France, it was licence-built in Yugoslavia and may still be in production in Serbia.

SPECIFICATION
Name: PA 15
Type: self-loading pistol
Calibre: 9-mm x 19 Parabellum
Weight: (empty) 1007 g
Dimensions: length 216 m; barrel length 136 mm
Muzzle velocity: 350 metres per second
Magazine capacity: 15-round box
Users: French armed forces, former French colonies

MANUFACTURE D'ARMES Automatiques de Bayonne, or MAB, are makers of a number of commercial and target pistols. Their **PA 15** pistol was chosen to equip the French armed forces in place of the government-designed and -manufactured single-action MAS model 1950.

GERMANY
P38 self-loading pistol

<p>

CARL WALTHER WAFFENFABRIK of Ulm is one of the most respected manufacturers of firearms in the world. In 1938 they developed a weapon known as the 'Armeepistole', which was adopted by the Wehrmacht as the **Pistole 38** or **P38**, as a replacement for the famous Luger.

One of the most influential military handguns of the 20th century, the P38 was more tolerant of poor ammunition and harsh conditions than the Luger, and the Walther's double-action trigger mechanism allowed a fast, if relatively inaccurate, shot. This feature has become very popular, and most modern service pistol designs are double-action.

P38s were prized war booty. A French resistance fighter uses a captured example to guard German officers during the liberation of Paris in 1944.

In front-line service since before World War II, the Walther P38 is still popular as a defence weapon. Its longevity testifies to its excellence as a combat pistol.

The P38 is still manufactured today, although modern versions use a lighter alloy frame than the all-steel frame of the wartime pistol. It has been used by the German army since its reconstitution in the 1950s; it is known there as the **Pistole 1** or **P1**.

SPECIFICATION

Name: P1 or P38
Type: self-loading pistol
Calibre: 9-mm x 19 Parabellum
Weight: (empty) 772 g
Dimensions: length 218 mm; barrel length 124 mm
Muzzle velocity: 350 metres per second
Magazine capacity: 8-round box
Users: Chile, Germany, Norway, Portugal, and other armed forces

The original P38 had a solid steel frame. Current military P1s and commercial P38s make use of alloy frames, which are lighter and cheaper to produce.

PPK self-loading pistol

A S THE NAME IMPLIES, Walther designed the **Polizei Pistole** or **PP** to arm uniformed policemen. Originally chambered in 7.65-mm or.32 Colt, it appeared in a variety of calibres including 9-mm Short (.38 Colt) and .22 Long Rifle. A smaller version appeared in 1931. Called the **Polizei Pistole Kriminal** or **PPK**, it was designed for concealed carry by detectives.

PPs and PPKs are well-made double-action blowback pistols, which have had a great deal of influence on gun designers all over the world. They are available in several different calibres, but all are distinguished by a lack of stopping power.

PPKs had a reputation for reliability, which was badly dented in the UK when a police officer guarding Princess Anne had a stoppage on the first round during a kidnap attempt in the 1970s. However, a faulty magazine was to blame, and the PPK will be around for some time to come.

Top: The neat and handy Walther PP and the even smaller PPK are among the most widely used pocket pistols in the world. They are ideal for concealed carry by plain-clothes detectives and bodyguards.

Inset: The design of the PP, the first truly successful double-action self-loading pistol, had a great influence on post-war handgun design, and copies of the Walthers have been made around the world.

SPECIFICATION

Name: PPK
Type: self-loading pistol
Calibre: 7.65-mm or 9-mm Short (9 x 17-mm)
Weight: (empty) 568 g
Dimensions: length 155 mm; barrel length 86 mm
Muzzle velocity: (7.65-mm) 280 metres per second
Magazine capacity: 7-round box
Users: in worldwide use by armed forces, police forces and as a personal protection weapon

The Walther PPK was a smaller version of the original police pistol, and was designed for concealed carry by detectives.

GERMANY
P5 self-loading pistol

The Walther P5 is essentially an updated P38, with a double-action trigger and improved safety.

GOOD THOUGH THE P38 has been, it is still an old design, and lacks many of the safety features now seen as essential by experienced gun users.

In the 1970s, Walther was asked to produce an updated P38 which would meet the exacting safety requirements demanded by the West German police. They came up with the **Pistole 5**, or **P5**.

The P5 uses the well-tried locking mechanism from the P38. It can be fired single-action by thumb-cocking the hammer, or double-action after releasing the de-cocking lever on the side. Its most notable safety feature is that the firing pin is kept out of line with the hammer unless the trigger is pulled. Even if the hammer is released other than by trigger pull, the firing pin will not be struck. The hammer itself has a safety notch which can be engaged to prevent firing, and as a final safety measure none of the pistol's working parts will operate unless the slide is fully closed and the barrel locked in place.

Getting four different safety features into what is a relatively small pistol was a major design accomplishment, but it has paid dividends for the firer. The P5 is easy to aim and shoot, and its smoother lines mean that there is less to get caught up in clothing than with the preceding P38. It is a very handy weapon which has been widely exported to the USA and South America, and is employed by German and Dutch police forces.

SPECIFICATION
Name: P5
Type: self-loading pistol
Calibre: 9-mm x 19 Parabellum
Weight: (empty) 795 g
Dimensions: length 180 mm; barrel length 90 mm
Muzzle velocity: 350 metres per second
Magazine capacity: 8-round box
Users: German police, Netherlands police, Nigeria, Portugal, US police forces, and various South American armies

GERMANY
P-88 self-loading pistol

The P-88 is the first Walther design to use the popular Colt-Browning locking system.

THE US ARMY HAS HAD an enormous influence on modern pistol design. Its programme to replace the venerable Colt .45 saw most major manufacturers producing advanced new weapons to the US Army specification, in the hope of winning the biggest handgun order in the world. The Walther **P-88** is one such pistol.

The P-88 differs radically from previous Walther designs both in looks and internally. It employs a modified Colt-Browning locking system, as opposed to the locking wedge used on the P38, and retains the double-action mechanism and ambidextrous de-cocking lever introduced on the P5, together with the multiple safety features. These ensure that the only way to fire the weapon is by pulling on the trigger, as the firing pin cannot be pushed forwards by dropping the pistol or otherwise delivering an accidental blow to the frame.

The chunky grip is filled with a large-capacity magazine which is locked and released by the now-standard thumb-operated ambidextrous magazine release catch. It is normally supplied in NATO standard 9-mm x 19 Parabellum calibre, but can also be chambered for the more powerful 9 x 21-mm target-shooting round.

SPECIFICATION
Name: P-88
Type: self-loading pistol
Calibre: 9-mm x 19 Parabellum
Weight: (empty) 900 g
Dimensions: length 187 mm; barrel length 102 mm
Muzzle velocity: 350 metres per second
Magazine capacity: 15-round box
Users: some military and police forces in Europe and the USA

GERMANY
HK4 self-loading pistol

The HK4 comes equipped with four barrels and sets of working parts, and can easily be converted from .22LR to 6.35-mm, 7.65-mm, or 9-mm Short calibres.

ACP (9-mm Short). It proved popular, achieving considerable commercial success.

Although primarily a concealed-carry self-defence weapon, the smaller rounds the HK4 is chambered to fire lack stopping power. The .22 LR is really too small for self-defence, though it makes an effective and economical training round. It also has a more sinister application, as a close-range assassination round.

T HE **HK4** IS ONE OF THE BEST blowback pistols ever designed. Built by Heckler & Koch, it is an updated version of the revolutionary Mauser Model HSc double-action auto introduced in 1940.

The HK4 was sold as a four-calibre package all in one gun, so the weapon comes complete with barrels and springs for .22 LR, .25 ACP, .32 ACP and .380

SPECIFICATION
Name: HK4
Type: self-loading pistol
Calibre: .22 long rifle, 6.35-mm (.25 Colt), 7.65-mm (.32 Colt), or 9-mm short (.380 Colt)
Weight: (empty) 520 g
Dimensions: length 157 mm; barrel length 85 mm
Muzzle velocity: (9 mm Short) 295 metres per second
Magazine capacity: 7- or 8-round box
Users: no longer manufactured, but in widespread use as a personal protection weapon

---

GERMANY
P7 self-loading pistol

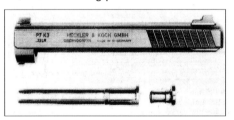

The pocket-sized K3 variant of the P7 can be quickly converted to fire .22LR rounds simply by changing the slide, barrel and firing pin.

The P7 requires the firer to squeeze to cock the weapon. After the first pressure, it requires little effort to hold the cocking device back, but as soon as the grip is released the gun becomes safe.

D ESIGNED BY HECKLER & KOCH for the police market and originally known as the **PSP**, the **P7** is instantly recognisable thanks to the prominent squeeze cocking device on the front of the grip. This cocks the firing pin ready for the first shot and, when released, de-cocks the pin. Thus, there is no way to discharge the gun unless it is actually in the shooter's hand

The P7 is very reliable, being much less liable to misfeeds than most other magazine pistols. Current variants include the **P7M13**, with a 13-round magazine and the original **P7M8** with eight rounds. The **P7K3** is a simpler pocket version which fires less powerful 9-mm Short rounds. Most interesting are the **P7M7** and the **P7M10**, intended for the American market; these are chambered for .45 ACP and .40 S&W, and use a hydraulic recoil system.

The standard P7 uses a gas-operated delayed-blowback operating system, rather like that found in the Austrian Steyr GB pistol.

SPECIFICATION
Name: P7M13
Type: self-loading pistol
Calibre: 9-mm x 19 Parabellum
Weight: (empty) 800 g
Dimensions: length 171 mm; barrel length 105 mm
Muzzle velocity: 351 metres per second
Magazine capacity: 13-round box
Users: German army and special forces, US police forces, military and police forces in Europe, Asia, and South America

GERMANY

P9 self-loading pistol

CONCEIVED AS A LIGHTWEIGHT military pistol able to fire full-power 9-mm rounds, the Heckler & Koch **P9** is unusual in that it uses the famous Heckler & Koch roller-locked delayed blowback system originally developed for the G3 rifle. This is much more complex than is usually encountered in a pistol, but gives the action immense strength. The barrel is also unusual in having a 'polygonal bore': the grooves of the rifling are round-edged and merge into the bore, which the manufacturers claim reduces bullet deformation and increases muzzle velocity and accuracy.

The P9 was originally produced as a single-action weapon, but the later **P9S** is double-action. The gun is also produced in .45 ACP for the American market and was briefly produced in 7.65-mm Parabellum. It is used by German and many other police forces and military units

Capable of exceptional accuracy, the P9 is offered in several competition versions as well as the basic police model seen here.

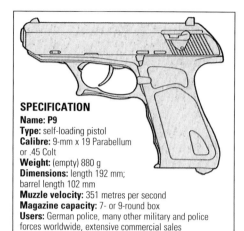

SPECIFICATION
Name: P9
Type: self-loading pistol
Calibre: 9-mm x 19 Parabellum or .45 Colt
Weight: (empty) 880 g
Dimensions: length 192 mm; barrel length 102 mm
Muzzle velocity: 351 metres per second
Magazine capacity: 7- or 9-round box
Users: German police, many other military and police forces worldwide, extensive commercial sales

---

ISRAEL

Desert Eagle self-loading pistol

MANUFACTURED IN ISRAEL by IMI, the immensely powerful **Desert Eagle** was designed in the USA as one of the first semi-automatic pistols capable of handling high-power revolver rounds. It is available in .357 and .44 Magnum as well as .41 and the awesome .50 calibre Action Express.

To handle the heavy-duty ammunition, the Desert Eagle is made from high-quality steels, though an aluminium frame is also available. The powerful weapon is gas-operated and has a rotating bolt – features more commonly found on rifles. The trigger is adjustable, and several different types of sight can be fitted. The trigger guard is shaped to be fired from a two-handed grip.

The Desert Eagle is too powerful for normal military use, but its power makes the weapon a natural candidate for special operations. It has been a great success commercially.

SPECIFICATION
Name: Desert Eagle
Type: self-loading pistol
Calibre: .357 or .44 Magnum; .41 or .50 Action Express
Weight: (empty) 1760 g
Dimensions: length 260 mm; barrel length 152 mm
Muzzle velocity: 436 metres per second (.357 Magnum)
Magazine capacity: 9-round box
Users: wide commercial ownership

Model 92 self-loading pistol

THE ITALIAN FIRM OF BERETTA is one of the oldest gun manufacturers in the world, noted for the quality of its products. Its biggest-selling handgun, first introduced in 1976, is the **Model 92**. This large-magazine-capacity 9-mm semi-automatic is built in at least a dozen variants.

The Model 92 has become a controversial weapon since the **Model 92F** won the protracted trials conducted by the US Army to select a replacement for the venerable Colt M1911A1. Adopted by the US Army under the designation **M9**, the Beretta has had some teething problems – doubts have been voiced about its long-term durability, and at one stage deliveries fell far behind schedule.

A handsome and accurate gun, it was popularised as a civilian weapon in the USA by the movie *Lethal Weapon*. In spite of the problems it has

Used extensively by the Italian armed forces, the Beretta Model 92 was thoroughly re-worked to meet US requirements. As the Model 92F it won the US Department of Defense's protracted competition to find a replacement for the long-serving Colt Model 1911.

faced, the adoption of the Model 92 by the US Armed forces has influenced other organisations, notably the French Gendarmerie, to choose the weapon as their service pistol.

SPECIFICATION

Name: Model 92
Type: self-loading pistol
Calibre: 9-mm x 19 Parabellum
Weight: (empty) 950 g
Dimensions: length 217 mm; barrel length 125 mm
Muzzle velocity: 390 metres per second
Magazine capacity: 15-round box
Users: Italian armed forces, Italian police; US Army, Navy, Marine Corps, Air Force, Coast Guard; French Gendarmerie Nationale; other military and law enforcement agencies around the world

The Model 92 has the characteristic Beretta open-topped slide. It has been developed into several variants, including a compact gun firing a low-power cartridge.

The American Beretta 92 has a modified trigger guard and extended base to facilitate a two-handed grip. It can also be fitted with a long barrel and counterweight for target shooting.

ITALY

RF 83 revolver

LUIGI FRANCHI IS ANOTHER long-established firm of Italian gunmakers. The company's **Model RF 83 Service** is a very good Colt Python copy with a 102-mm barrel and a smooth double action. As with all revolvers, RF83s are not used as standard military issue, requiring more skill on the part of the shooter than self-loading pistols. But they are suitable for special operations and police work, where more time is available for training.

The Franchi is a conventional solid-frame double-action revolver with a swing-out cylinder. Built to very high standards, it is manufactured from hard-wearing nickel-chrome-molybdenum steel. Similar to the latest Ruger revolvers, the RF 83 does not have any of the Ruger's innovative takedown system, and requires the removal of a conventional side plate for access to the lock work.

The RF 83 series is also available in **Compact**, **Standard** and **Target** versions, differing primarily in barrel length and types of sights fitted. The Target model is available with a 152-mm barrel and adjustable sights. The only drawback with these excellent revolvers is that they will only fire .38 Specials, and not powerful Magnum rounds.

SPECIFICATION
Name: RF 83 Service
Type: revolver
Calibre: .38 Special
Weight: (empty) 800 g
Dimensions: length 230 mm; barrel length 101 mm
Muzzle velocity: 260 metres per second
Magazine capacity: 6-round cylinder
Users: some police forces and wide commercial sales

Franchi's RF 83 is a high-quality revolver suitable for police work. It is available with a short barrel and plain sights, or a long barrel with target sights as well as in the 101-mm service version depicted here.

SPAIN

Falcon self-loading pistol

ASTRA IS ONE OF A NUMBER of weapons makers from the Basque area of Spain, one of Europe's traditional arms-manufacturing regions. The company has manufactured many modern handguns, from .38, .357 Magnum and .44 Magnum calibre revolvers through the Model 80, which resembles the Swiss SIG P220 self-loading pistol, right down to the Model 60, a PPK-sized pocket pistol and the even smaller Cub. Firing the 6.35-mm (0.25-in) Auto Colt round, the Cub lacks the power to be a front-line military weapon, but its small size makes it easy to conceal and it can be used as a back-up weapon.

But the Astra **Falcon** is the sole survivor in production of the family of handguns that made Astra famous. The pistol is of simple and robust design, with origins dating back to the Campo-Giro pistol of 1913. Easily identifiable in these days of rectangular slides, the round-barrel weapon was for decades the Spanish army's standard service sidearm. It is a single-action pistol which has an external hammer and fixed sights. The magazine release button is in the grip.

The Falcon has been distributed throughout Europe for civilian and police use, as well as being issued as a service pistol in Spain.

The Astra Cub is a tiny gun which lacks stopping power, but it has a place in clandestine work, being very small and easy to conceal.

SPECIFICATION
Name: Falcon
Type: self-loading pistol
Calibre: 9-mm Short or 7.65-mm (.32 Colt)
Weight: (empty) 646 g
Dimensions: length 164 mm; barrel length 101 mm
Muzzle velocity: 300 metres per second
Magazine capacity: 7- or 8-round box
Users: may still be found in Spanish service, and some commercial sales

The Astra Falcon looks a little old-fashioned to modern eyes, possibly because its basic design dates back to before World War I.

P220 self-loading pistol

THE SWISS COMPANY SIG – Schweizerische Industrie-Gesellschaft – makes some of the world's best firearms. Swiss export regulations being very tough, weapons for export are often manufactured in Germany by J.P. Sauer & Sohn.

SIG's export success is founded on a range of pistols based on the **P220**, which appeared in the 1970s. It employs the same sort of locking cam as the Browning, but locks into the slide by using the enlarged chamber of the barrel to engage a wide ejection slot in the slide: a simple idea and a robust arrangement.

Despite the extensive use of metal stampings and an aluminium frame designed to keep down weight and cost, the excellent build quality of SIG pistols makes them expensive. However, their high standard of manufacture is reflected in a good record of safety and reliability. The P220 handles

German policewomen practise their skills on the range, armed with P6 pistols. This is the local designation for the SIG P225, a compact version of the P220. As with all SIGs, the pistols are as well crafted as a Swiss watch.

well, is easy to strip and maintain, and is available in a variety of calibres. As a result, SIGs have become popular with law enforcement organisations in the USA and special forces units worldwide.

The P220 is in service with the Swiss army, by whom it is designated Pistole 75. As a result, it is sometimes known as the SIG Model 75.

SPECIFICATION
Name: P220
Type: self-loading pistol
Calibre: 9-mm x 19 Parabellum (7.65-mm Parabellum, .45 Colt, .38 Super also manufactured)
Weight: (empty) 830 g
Dimensions: length 198 mm; barrel length 112 mm
Muzzle velocity: (9 mm) 345 metres per second
Magazine capacity: 9-round box
Users: Swiss army, Swiss police, US police forces, several undisclosed special forces units

SWITZERLAND
P226 self-loading pistol

About 80 per cent of the P226's parts are common to either the P220 or the P225. According to the company, the P226 is "the best pistol we have ever produced."

The P226 was developed for the infamous US joint services pistol trials. It easily met the demanding American specification, reportedly turning in the best performance of all the contenders. However, SIGs are costly, and the P226 was beaten to the contract by the much cheaper Beretta Model 92.

Testimony to the P226's effectiveness is provided by its adoption by the FBI and Britain's elite Special Air Service. The FBI load their pistols with Olin subsonic loads incorporating 147-grain soft-nose bullets. These do not overpenetrate like fully-jacketed 115-grain military loads, and still allow magazine capacity to be double that of a .45 pistol.

SPECIFICATION
Name: P226
Type: self-loading pistol
Calibre: 9-mm x 19 Parabellum
Weight: (empty) 750 g
Dimensions: length 196 mm; barrel length 112 mm
Muzzle velocity: 350 metres per second
Magazine capacity: 15- or 20- round box
Users: police and special forces worldwide, including Swiss police, German police, British SAS, FBI, many US police forces

IN THE 1980S, THE SWISS SIG COMPANY developed the **P225**. This was a slightly smaller pistol than the related P220, and although similar in operation it has added safety features, ensuring that a shot could only be fired by the deliberate pulling of the trigger. In the late 1980s, the company went on to introduce the **P226**. This was a new weapon combining parts from the P220 and P225.

SWITZERLAND
P228 self-loading pistol

THE LATEST IN THE FAMILY of pistols derived from the SIG P220, the **P228** is a successful attempt to combine a compact pistol with a high magazine capacity. It is equipped with excellent three-dot combat sights, and double- and single-action are possible. Manually-locked and recoil-operated, it is almost two centimetres shorter than the P220, but can carry a full 13 rounds of 9-mm Parabellum. The magazine catch can be mounted either left or right, depending on preference. The more slender grip and an optional short trigger reduces the overall bulk so that someone with small hands can manage the P228 quite comfortably – which is not always the case with modern pistols.

With an eye to the American police market, a version of the P228 with a slide of slightly modified shape is also being offered in .40 S&W calibre, under the designation **P229**. Also available in stainless steel finish, it is now being marketed in 9-mm calibre.

The **P239** is an even more recent SIG design. Smaller than the P229, it has been designed specifically with women in mind, since they are serving in increasing numbers in world armies. It sacrifices magazine capacity – down to seven or eight rounds – for a smaller, thinner butt which is much easier for small-handed people to use.

SPECIFICATION
Name: P228
Type: self-loading pistol
Calibre: 9-mm x 19 Parabellum
Weight: (empty) 830 g
Dimensions: length 180 mm; barrel length 98 mm
Muzzle velocity: 340 metres per second
Magazine capacity: 13-round box
Users: police and special forces

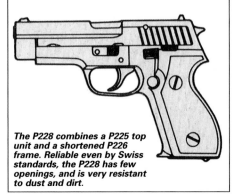

The P228 combines a P225 top unit and a shortened P226 frame. Reliable even by Swiss standards, the P228 has few openings, and is very resistant to dust and dirt.

M1911A1 self-loading pistol

IT IS A 20TH-CENTURY CLASSIC. Adopted by the US Army before World War I, the Colt **Model 1911** was designed by John Browning. Its design was enormously influential, and the Colt-Browning operating system has been imitated by manufacturers all over the world. It is still in production, and new variants appear regularly.

Although supplanted by the modern Beretta M9

Another war, and a very different enemy. An American 'tunnel rat' in Vietnam prepares to enter a Viet Cong bunker. But his weapon, now with more than 50 years' service, is still the trusty Colt.

First seeing military action against bandits on the Mexican border, the Model 1911 Colt has been used in every American war since then. Incredibly sturdy and hard-hitting, it remains in production although replaced in US service by the Beretta 92.

in 9-mm calibre, the Colt is still in service with US forces. Indeed, many units destined for the war with Iraq preferred to take their old Colt pistols to the Gulf.

The Colt M1911 has become the handgun by which all others are judged in the USA, where it is believed that the .45 cartridge has the advantage in stopping power over the smaller 9-mm Parabellum round which is standard in most of the rest of the world.

SPECIFICATION
Name: Model 1911A1
Type: self-loading pistol
Calibre: .45 ACP
Weight: (empty) 1130 g
Dimensions: length 219 mm; barrel length 127 mm
Muzzle velocity: 250 metres per second
Magazine capacity: 8-round box
Users: US armed forces, almost every country in South and Central America, Fiji, Iran, Korea, Liberia, Philippines, Taiwan, Zimbabwe

USA
Python revolver

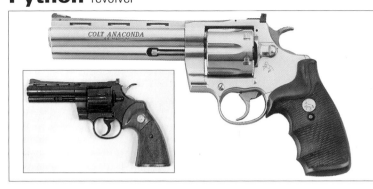

Not strictly a military weapon – it is far too expensive – the Colt Python (inset) makes an admirable police and security revolver to those who can afford it. It has been joined by the even more powerful Colt Anaconda, which fires the awesome .44 Magnum round.

ARGUABLY THE BEST production revolver in the world, the Colt **Python** has an excellent double-action operation and the standard of workmanship is very high. The weapon is extremely heavy-duty and will fire full-power .357 Magnum factory loads throughout its service life.

As with most revolvers, the Python lacks the high magazine capacity of self-loading pistols, but is far more robust. To security personnel, its immense power makes up for the lack of capacity. The only real trouble is the price; many military equipment or police force budgets simply cannot afford it.

SPECIFICATION
Name: Python
Type: revolver
Calibre: .357 Magnum
Weight: (empty) 1116 g with 152-mm barrel
Dimensions: length 255 mm with 102-mm barrel; barrel length 64 mm, 102 mm, 152 mm, or 203 mm
Muzzle velocity: 450 metres per second
Magazine capacity: 6-round cylinder
Users: wide commercial sales, some police and military police units

---

USA
Lawman revolver

Colt has been making revolvers since the 1830s. The Colt Lawman, seen here with a short-barrelled Colt Cobra, is the product of more than a century of development and experience.

a powerful but more compact revolver than the Trooper Mk 5. The Lawman is very solidly constructed and moderately priced, and is available in blue nickel or Colt Guard finishes in 51- or 102-mm barrel lengths.

Another popular Colt is the **Cobra,** a lighter and more modern weapon. Similar in design to the very expensive Python, the Cobra was designed to fire the .38 Special round. Simpler to use and requiring less expertise to master than the more powerful Magnum, the .38 Special has been a standard police and security round since the 1900s. Good accuracy and controllable recoil mean that is still popular.

THE COLT **TROOPER** IS A LARGE revolver from the 1950s. Designed for the police market, it was built in a variety of calibres and barrel lengths. Solidly-built and very reliable, the trooper sold extensively to American police forces.

The Trooper was succeeded by the **Lawman.** This is a medium-frame bull-barrelled .357 Magnum revolver with fixed sights. It handles well and has a good double action with a short hammer throw, and it is obviously built to satisfy a police requirement for

SPECIFICATION
Name: Lawman Mk III
Type: security revolver
Calibre: .357 Magnum
Weight: (empty) 1022g
Dimensions: length 235 mm; barrel 51 mm or 102 mm
Muzzle velocity: 430 metres per second
Magazine capacity: 6-round cylinder
Users: US armed forces police and security units, US police forces, other security forces

Speed-Six revolver

US Air Force police practise getting their Ruger service revolvers into action quickly.

reliable weapons, many of whose working parts are manufactured from stainless steel. The Speed-Six has been adopted for US military use under the designation GS-32N. Although replaced in production by revolvers of more modern design, the weapons are still in widespread use.

SPECIFICATION

Name: Speed-Six
Type: revolver
Calibre: 9-mm, .38 Special, or .357 Magnum
Weight: (empty) 964 g
Dimensions: length 197 mm; barrel length 70 mm (also made with 102 mm barrels)
Muzzle velocity: 260 metres per second with .38 Special
Magazine capacity: 6-round cylinder
Users: US armed forces, police, and government agencies

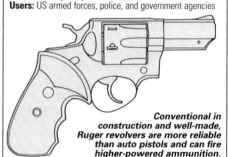

Conventional in construction and well-made, Ruger revolvers are more reliable than auto pistols and can fire higher-powered ammunition.

STURM, RUGER AND COMPANY has been making firearms since 1949. Some of the company's products are destined for private hands, but it also produces weapons for the military and police market.

Ruger revolvers are almost exclusively used by military police and security units. since they are the only people whose role requires familiarity with, and can devote the time to training in, the handling of such powerful weapons.

The Ruger **Speed-Six** Revolver and the closely related **Service-Six** and **Security-Six** are rugged,

Ruger GP 100 revolver

The Ruger GP 100 is an exceptionally smooth-handling revolver, although as with all weapons of the type its recoil makes it much more of a handful than any self-loading pistol.

easier to strip and clean. The weapon is very accurate and has an exceptionally smooth double action straight out of the box.

The **SP101** is a much smaller five-shot weapon along the same lines, designed to fire the less powerful .38 Special round, although versions are available in other calibres.

SPECIFICATION

Name: GP 100
Type: revolver
Calibre: .357 Magnum
Weight: (empty) 1247 g with 152-mm barrel
Dimensions: length 235 mm; barrel length 102 mm (also made with 70-mm barrels)
Muzzle velocity: 260 metres per second with .38 Special
Magazine capacity: 6-round cylinder
Users: US police; government and other security forces

THE **GP 100** IS RUGER'S replacement in the police pistol market for the successful Speed-Six range. The long ejector shroud gives a slightly muzzle-heavy feel that gives good point qualities and cuts down felt recoil; the composite grips of wood and rubber work very well; and the take-down has been improved, making the revolver even

USA

Smith & Wesson 1006 self-loading pistol

SMITH & WESSON IS well known for its revolvers, but the company also produces a thoroughly modern range of semi-automatic pistols.

All Smith & Wesson pistols are described by their four-number designation. Those starting in 39, 59, or 69 are 9-mm weapons. Those starting in 10, 40, or 45 are in calibre 10-mm, .40 S&W, or .45 Colt. The third number denotes size and the last figure indicates from what it is made – '0' indicates a standard weapon, and '6' stands for stainless steel.

The 10-mm cartridge was developed by practical pistol shooters in the USA who wanted a hard-hitting cartridge superior to the .45 ACP. FBI interest in the 10-mm round led to collaborative work with Smith & Wesson and the introduction of the **Model 1006** in 1990. With Novak sights, combat grips and double-action facility, it is a very powerful handgun indeed. The FBI now uses a developed version known as the **Model 1076,** which has a de-cocking lever instead of a slide-mounted safety.

Along with the 10-mm round, Smith & Wesson has also achieved success with the .40 S&W calibre, a round of similar power and performance but as an imperial measure, more in tune with American preferences.

SPECIFICATION
Name: Model 1006
Type: self-loading pistol
Calibre: 10-mm
Weight: (empty) 1185 g
Dimensions: length 216 mm; barrel length 127 mm
Muzzle velocity: 370 metres per second
Magazine capacity: 9-round box
Users: FBI and other security organisations

All third-generation Smith & Wesson pistols like the Model 1006 were designed after extensive consultation with the police officers and security men who use the guns.

USSR

TT-33 self-loading pistol

Standard Red Army self-loading pistols during World War II, Tokarevs were widely exported and, although obsolete, may still be found in use in many former Soviet client states.

Although not well made or finished, the Tokarev is a typically robust Soviet design, able to take hard knocks but still keep functioning. Although simple by modern standards – It has no safety catch – and long replaced in the armies of the former Soviet states, the reliable Tokarev may still be encountered all over the world.

SPECIFICATION
Name: TT 33
Type: self-loading pistol
Calibre: 7.62-mm x 25 (7.62-mm Soviet)
Weight: (empty) 830 g
Dimensions: length 193 mm; barrel length 116 mm

Muzzle velocity:
418 metres per second
Magazine capacity:
8-round box
Users: former Soviet clients all over the world

The TT-33 is based on the American Model 1911 Colt, but simplified for ease of manufacture and use.

DESIGNED BY TOKAREV in the 1920s, the **Pistolet Obr 1933g Tul'skiy Tokarev,** or **TT 33** was the service pistol of the Soviet army and its client states from 1933 until the 1950s.

Using Browning's swinging-link locking system, the Tokarev is chambered for the Soviet 7.62 x 25-mm cartridge. This is almost identical dimensionally to the high-powered 7.63 Mauser Export round, which the Tokarev will fire without much problem.

Makarov self-loading pistol

The Makarov is smaller and less powerful than the preceding Tokarev, but it is much easier to handle and more practical as a military sidearm.

Makarovs are used in the armies of ex-Soviet republics, and can be found in most former Warsaw Pact and former Soviet client states. Large numbers have been manufactured in China, where it is known as the **Type 59**. Makarovs were also built in Poland as the **P-64** and in the former German Democratic Republic as the **Pistole M**. All three countries also made the special Makarov ammunition.

ALTHOUGH THE SOVIET ARMY never considered the pistol to be a practical military weapon, they still issued handguns in large numbers for personal protection. The **Pistolet Makarova** or **PM** has been the standard Soviet service pistol from the 1950s onwards, after it had replaced the more powerful but more difficult-to-control Tokarev. It was first reported by Western intelligence agencies in the early 1960s.

The small and handy Makarov is essentially an enlarged copy of the influential pre-war German police pistol, the Walther PP, design of which dated back to the 1920s. Unlike the Walther, however, the Makarov is chambered for the Soviet 9 x 18-mm pistol cartridge, which is intermediate between the 9-mm Short (or .38 Colt) and the more powerful 9-mm Parabellum used in the West. The cartridge appears to have been based on a World War II German cartridge known as Ultra.

The Makarov is a straightforward blowback pistol, reasonably well-manufactured from high-quality steels, although the trigger pull is usually awful. But even though it is fairly tough and reliable, by Western standards it remains a very basic weapon, hardly comparable to a pre-war Browning, let alone a modern SIG.

SPECIFICATION

Name: PM
Type: self-loading pistol
Calibre: 9-mm x 18 Soviet
Weight: (empty) 720 g
Dimensions: length 160 mm; barrel length 98 mm
Muzzle velocity: 325 metres per second
Magazine capacity: 8-round box
Users: most former Soviet and Warsaw Pact armies, China, former Soviet client states

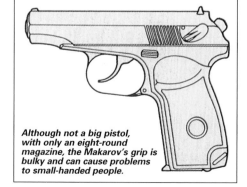

Although not a big pistol, with only an eight-round magazine, the Makarov's grip is bulky and can cause problems to small-handed people.

SUB-MACHINE GUNS

AUSTRALIA
F1 sub-machine gun

with short-barrelled weapons.

Simple and effective, the F1 in its prototype **X3** form performed extremely well in the Mekong Delta during the Vietnam War.

The top-loading magazine is unique to the F1 among modern sub-machine guns.

SPECIFICATION
Name: F1
Type: sub-machine gun
Calibre: 9-mm x 19 Parabellum
Weight: empty 3.27 kg
Dimensions: length 714 mm; barrel length 213 mm
Muzzle velocity: 400 metres per second
Effective range: 200 m
Rate of fire: 600-640 rpm (cyclic)
Magazine: 34-round box
Users: Australian Defence Forces

REPLACING THE VERY POPULAR World War II vintage Owen Gun in Australian service, the **F1** retains the uniquely Australian feature of a top-loading magazine.

Similar but not identical to the Sterling, the F1 uses the same pistol grip as that used on the L1A1 self-loading rifle, and the cocking handle also duplicates the position and action of the FN design.

A sling swivel bracket on the barrel shroud acts as a safety feature in preventing the hand getting too close to the muzzle, which is a common mishap

---

ARGENTINA
FMK-3 sub-machine gun

With a design heavily influenced by the Israeli Uzi, the FMK-3 is a simply-manufactured but fairly effective military sub-machine gun.

THE **FMK-3** IS MANUFACTURED by Fabrica Militar de Armas Portatiles `Domingo Matheu' of Argentina. Originally known as the **PA3-DM**, it is one of a long series of sub-machine gun designs produced by the concern in the years since World War II. The immediate predecessor was the **PAM 2**, which was little more than a copy of the American M3A1 'Grease Gun', only built in 9-mm calibre. The FMK-3 shares little with the preceding weapon other than the fact that it has a sliding wire butt copied from the M3, replacing the fixed plastic butt originally supplied.

The FMK-3 is manufactured from pressed steel components, having a decidedly 'under-the-counter' appearance, but it is nonetheless an effective weapon. It is a typical blowback-operated sub-machine gun of basic modern design. It has a wrap-around bolt, first used on the Czech vz 23 and the hugely influential Israeli Uzi. The arrangement provides a number of advantages; by wrapping the bolt around the barrel, the overall length can be reduced by a considerable margin, making the weapon much

shorter and handier. The 40-round magazine is housed in the pistol grip in the fashion of the Uzi, which improves the balance and makes reloading easier, especially in the dark. The cocking handle is mounted well forward on the left side, but can be operated by either hand. The barrel screws onto the front of the tubular receiver, and it can also be adapted to mount a device for launching grenades.

The FMK-3 has not been exported. A relatively small number were used during the Falklands war, and many captured examples have found their way into British regimental museums.

SPECIFICATION
Name: FMK-3
Type: sub-machine gun
Calibre: 9-mm x 19 Parabellum
Weight: empty 3.76 kg
Dimensions: length 520 mm, butt retracted; barrel length 290 mm
Muzzle velocity: 400 metres per second
Effective range: 150 m
Rate of fire: 600 rpm (cyclic)
Magazine: 40-round box
Users: Argentine forces

AUSTRIA
MPi 69 sub-machine gun

The MPi 69 is a handy weapon with a number of unusual handling features.

way back gives full-auto fire.

Early models were cocked by pulling back on the permanently-attached sling, but the later **MPi 81** has a conventional cocking lever.

Although influenced externally by the Uzi – from a distance it looks very similar to the Israeli gun – the Steyr MPi 69 is a very different weapon.

THE STEYR **MPi 69** LOOKS like an Uzi clone, with a similar boxy body, and its magazine feeds through the pistol grip. But the Steyr is not a copy, and differs internally.

The MPi 69 has a number of unusual features. It has no selector lever. A cross-bolt safety has three positions: pressed to the right by the thumb, it shows a white 'S' for safe. Pressed to the left, a red 'F' shows, releasing the trigger. First trigger pressure fires single-shot, and pulling the trigger all the

SPECIFICATION
Name: MPi 69
Type: sub-machine gun
Calibre: 9-mm x 19 Parabellum
Weight: 3.13 kg
Dimensions: length 465 mm, butt retracted; barrel length 260 mm
Muzzle velocity: 381 metres per second
Effective range: 150 m
Rate of fire: 550 rpm (cyclic)
Magazine: 25- or 32-round box
Users: a number of military and police forces

AUSTRIA
AUG 9 Para sub-machine gun

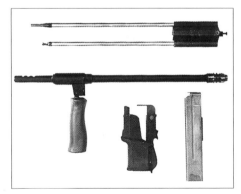

The AUG 9, a 9-mm version of the AUG, blurs the distinction between rifles and SMGs. It can be changed from one to the other simply by changing the barrel, bolt group, magazine adaptor and magazine (right).

IF YOU TAKE AN ASSAULT RIFLE and convert it to fire pistol rounds, it becomes indistinguishable from a sub-machine gun, especially when you fit a shorter barrel.

The Steyr AUG assault rifle can easily be converted into the **AUG 9 Para** sub-machine gun because of its modular construction. The stock and receiver remain the same, but the barrel is changed, and the bolt mechanism is exchanged for an unlocked blowback bolt unit. The resulting weapon fires from a closed bolt, and its 420-mm barrel and optical sight give remarkable accuracy out beyond 200 metres.

SPECIFICATION
Name: AUG 9 Para
Type: sub-machine gun
Calibre: 9-mm x 19 Parabellum
Weight: 3.3 kg
Dimensions: length 665 mm; barrel length 420 mm
Muzzle velocity: 400 metres per second
Effective range: 200 m
Rate of fire: 650-750 rpm (cyclic)
Magazine: 25- or 32-round box
Users: Austrian Cobra special forces units

CZECH REPUBLIC
Model 61 Skorpion machine pistol

result, a formidable close-quarters weapon, and its small size and ease of concealment make it a favourite of terrorist groups.

Best described as a machine pistol, the Skorpion is no bigger than a handgun.

SPECIFICATION
Name: Model 61 Skorpion
Type: machine pistol
Calibre: 7.65-mm x 17 (.32 ACP)
Weight: empty 1.59 kg
Dimensions: length 269 mm, butt retracted; barrel length 112 mm
Muzzle velocity: 317 metres per second
Effective range: 75 m
Rate of fire: 840 rpm (cyclic)
Magazine: 10- or 20-round box
Users: Czech and Slovak republics, former Yugoslav republics, Angola, Libya, Uganda; also used by terrorist and guerrilla groups

THE **MODEL 61 SKORPION** was designed for use by tank crews, signallers and other personnel who need more firepower than a pistol provides.

Firing 7.65-mm ammunition, its small bolt generates an unacceptably high rate of fire, so a spring-loaded weight is fitted into the butt as a rate reducer. However, the bouncing up and down this causes, added to the almost uncontrollable muzzle climb arising out of fully-automatic fire through such a small weapon, means that the Skorpion sprays bullets about in a very alarming fashion. It is, as a

DENMARK
Madsen sub-machine gun

The Madsen is simple and tough, like most SMGs developed during and just after World War II.

together by the barrel nut. Field stripping is simplicity itself, since by unscrewing the barrel nut you can open the receiver like a suitcase, hinged at the rear, and remove the working parts.

The Model 46 was succeeded by the similar **Model 50**, **Model 53**, and the **Mk II**, the only selective-fire model, which could be supplied with a perforated barrel jacket.

Simple and reliable, the Madsen achieved considerable success on the export market and was adopted by military and paramilitary forces in South America and Asia.

THE FIRST SUB-MACHINE GUNS developed in the inter-war years were, like other small arms of the time, very highly engineered. During World War II, however, it became clear that short-range weapons need not be built to such exacting specifications; indeed, highly effective weapons like the British Sten gun and the American M3 'Grease Gun' looked as though they had been thrown together in a plumber's workshop. But for all their crude appearance, such guns were tough and reliable and were cheap to produce and repair.

Work on the Danish **Madsen** sub-machine gun began only months after the end of World War II. Using the production techniques pioneered by the British with the Sten gun and the Soviets with the PPS, the Dansk Industri Syndicat produced the first of a series of basically similar, brutally simple weapons built mostly from sheet metal stampings.

The **Madsen Model 46** has a square receiver that swings into two longitudinal halves, held

SPECIFICATION
Name: Madsen Model 46
Type: sub-machine gun
Calibre: 9-mm x 19 Parabellum
Weight: empty 3.2 kg
Dimensions: length 794 mm, stock extended; barrel length 198 mm
Muzzle velocity: 390 metres per second
Effective range: 150 m
Rate of fire: 550 rpm (cyclic)
Magazine: 32-round box
Users: Denmark, Brazil (built under licence), several Southeast Asian and South American forces

FINLAND
Jatimatic machine pistol

The Jati is a tiny weapon, not much bigger than a pistol, but thanks to its foldaway foregrip it is easily controllable even in fully automatic fire.

THE SUB-MACHINE GUN has come a long way in its relatively short lifespan. The futuristic-looking **Jatimatic** from Finland is typical of modern weapons, if a little smaller than most. Designed primarily as a very light weapon that is nevertheless easy to control, it succeeds in its aim as well as any weapon of its type.

Largely made from pressed steel for economy in manufacture, the Jatimatic is not much bigger than a handgun, and is best described as a machine pistol.

The weapon's 'bent' appearance stems from the fact that the bolt travels on an inclined plane angled up from the barrel. This also makes the weapon much simpler to control when firing full-auto. First trigger pressure gives single shots; further pressure against a spring stop produces automatic fire. The Jatimatic has a folding foregrip, which should be used whenever firing automatically. With a 20-round magazine the Jatimatic weighs less than two kilograms.

As with many modern firearms, the Finnish machine pistol has a range of optional extras and accessories. These included higher-capacity magazines, suppressors, and a high-tech 'red-dot' laser aiming device.

SPECIFICATION
Name: Jatimatic
Type: machine pistol
Calibre: 9-mm x 19 Parabellum
Weight: empty 1.65 kg
Dimensions: length 375 mm; barrel length 203 mm
Muzzle velocity: 360-400 metres per second
Effective range: 150 m
Rate of fire: 600-650 rpm (cyclic)
Magazine: 20- or 40-round box
Users: Finland, China (manufactured under licence), various commercial sales

---

FRANCE
MAS 38 sub-machine gun

The MAS 38 was a fairly good weapon, but its underpowered round meant that it never sold beyond the French-speaking world.

THE FRENCH FIREARMS INDUSTRY in the years after World War I was responsible for a number of curious, old-fashioned or unreliable weapons designs. However, just before World War II the Manufacture d'Armes de St Etienne introduced the **MAS Model 38** sub-machine gun. It was a workmanlike and effective design, with some advanced features.

Although made to a high standard, the MAS 38 does not incorporate any unnecessary parts, and is lighter than most of its contemporaries. Although close to a 'straight through' design with barrel and butt almost in line, the MAS 38 has a curious 'bent' profile. The barrel leaves the receiver at an angle; inside, the breech block travels at an angle to the bore. Although accurate and with a low recoil, the weapon was chambered for the unique French 7.65-mm *longue* cartridge rather than the by-then popular 9-mm Parabellum, and export sales were limited to French colonies.

The MAS 38 was in production when the French army was defeated in 1940, and the factory stayed in operation throughout the Vichy period and the subsequent German occupation.

After the war, when French forces became embroiled in a fierce guerrilla war in Indo-China, the MAS 38 was used alongside US-supplied Thompsons and its French successor, the MAT 49. Some of those captured by the Viet Minh were reportedly converted to fire the Soviet 7.62-mm x 25 pistol and SMG cartridge. The MAS Model 38 was used in both forms in Vietnam.

SPECIFICATION
Name: Mas 38
Type: sub-machine gun
Calibre: 7.65-mm *longue* (7.65-mm x 19.5)
Weight: empty 2.87 kg
Dimensions: length 734 mm; barrel length 224 mm
Muzzle velocity: 350 metres per second
Effective range: 150 m
Rate of fire: 600 rpm (cyclic)
Magazine: 32-round box
Users: obsolete, but may be found in Africa and Southeast Asia

FRANCE
MAT 49 sub-machine gun

The MAT 49 was first used in action in Indochina. These paratroopers at Dien Bien Phu were to soon lose their weapons to the Viet Minh when the beleaguered French fortress surrendered.

paratroopers or vehicle crew, and it has a sliding wire stock similar to that of the American M3 'Grease Gun'. Unusually, the head of the bolt enters an extension of the chamber, producing a wraparound barrel instead of a wraparound bolt. The MAT 49 is still in widespread use in French-speaking countries.

The conventional but solidly constructed MAT 49 may be encountered in any former French colony.

SPECIFICATION
Name: MAT 49
Type: sub-machine gun
Calibre: 9-mm x 19 Parabellum
Weight: empty 3.5 kg
Dimensions: length 460 mm, butt retracted; barrel length 228 mm
Muzzle velocity: 390 metres per second
Effective range: 150 m
Rate of fire: 600 rpm (cyclic)
Magazine: 20- or 32-round box
Users: France, former French colonies

IN THE YEARS FOLLOWING World War II the French army was equipped with a variety of sub-machine guns, mainly of British and American origin. The variety of calibres was confusing, so a new 9-mm sub-machine gun was developed by the Manufacture d'Armes de Tulle.

The **MAT 49** is an extremely robust SMG that proved reliable in France's colonial wars in Indo-China and in Algeria. The magazine swings forward to lie under the barrel, which makes it convenient for

---

GERMANY
MP-K and MP-L sub-machine gun

The Walther is a competent weapon, but has been overshadowed by competition from the more complex but more accurate Heckler & Koch MP5.

muzzle velocity, greater range and better accuracy. Both models have been widely exported to armies and police forces in South America.

The Walther fires from an open bolt. The wire stock folds forward so that the shoulder section can be used as a forward grip. Both models can be set for single-shot operation or fully automatic.

SPECIFICATION
Name: MP-K
Type: sub-machine gun
Calibre: 9 x 19 mm Parabellum
Weight: empty 2.82 kg
Dimensions: length 460 mm, butt retracted; barrel length 228 mm
Muzzle velocity: 390 metres per second
Effective range: 150 m
Rate of fire: 600 rpm (cyclic)
Magazine: 20- or 32-round box
Users: Germany, Brazil, Colombia, Mexico, Venezuela

ADOPTED BY THE WEST GERMAN police before the advent of the Heckler & Koch MP5, the simple blowback pressed-steel **MP** built by Walther is made in two versions. The standard **MP-L** has a 257-mm barrel, while the short **MP-K** version's barrel is only 171 mm long. The MP-K is more concealable, whereas the MP-L has a higher

MP5 sub-machine gun

THE HECKLER & KOCH **MP5** sub-machine gun is one of the most widely used weapons of its type. Although it is more complex and considerably more expensive than most other SMGs, it has become the weapon of choice for the world's special operations and hostage rescue units.

When the SAS stormed the Iranian Embassy in London in 1981, it was the first time TV viewers around the world had seen the MP5 in action. Airport guards and police officers in many countries have also been issued with selective-fire MP5s following a number of high-profile terrorist attacks in the early 1980s.

Firing from a closed bolt, the MP5 is probably the most accurate sub-machine gun in production today. It is manufactured in a number of variants. These include the **MP5 A2** which has a fixed stock, the

The MP5 appeared in a blaze of publicity during the storming of the Iranian Embassy in London by the British Army's elite SAS Regiment.

MP5 A3 with a telescoping metal stock, the short-barrelled **MP5K** designed for easy concealment, and the **MP5 SD** series, which incorporate built-in silencers. Most variants are also available with a three-round burst capability.

SPECIFICATION

Name: MP5 A2
Type: sub-machine gun
Calibre: 9-mm x 19 Parabellum
Weight: empty 2.55 kg
Dimensions: length 680 mm, fixed butt; barrel length 225 mm
Muzzle velocity: 400 metres per second
Effective range: 200 m
Rate of fire: 800 rpm (cyclic)
Magazine: 15- or 30- round box
Users: police and military forces in at least 30 countries

The MP5 is one of a large family of weapons made by Heckler & Koch which incorporates the company's roller locking system.

The MP5 A2 has a fixed butt. The MP5 A3 has a sliding metal stock which allows the user to reduce the length of the gun from 660 mm to 490 mm.

ISRAEL
Uzi sub-machine gun

South Africa is one of many nations to use the Uzi. First seeing widespread action with Israel during the 1956 Sinai war, it remains a highly effective design.

EVEN THOUGH ITS DESIGN dates back more than 40 years, the **Uzi** remains one of the most effective sub-machine guns available today. Named after designer Uziel Gal, the compact weapon was developed at a time when Israel was beset by enemies yet had little in the way of manufacturing facilities. As a result the gun is largely made from cheap pressed-steel parts.

The Uzi features a bolt that wraps around the barrel, first employed on the pre-war Model 23 sub-machine gun made in Czechoslovakia. Although of short overall dimensions, the Uzi has a barrel that is actually longer than that of more conventional weapons. The magazine's location in the pistol grip means that it is much easier to reload in the dark.

In military use the gun has gained an enviable reputation for reliability. The design has also fathered a series of smaller weapons, suitable for clandestine use. These include the **Mini-Uzi,** the **Micro-Uzi** and the **Uzi pistol**.

The Mini-Uzi is a smaller, lighter and even handier version of the original design.

SPECIFICATION
Name: Uzi
Type: sub-machine gun
Calibre: 9-mm x 19 Parabellum
Weight: empty 3.7 kg
Dimensions: length 470 mm, stock retracted ; barrel length 260 mm
Muzzle velocity: 400 metres per second
Effective range: 200 m
Rate of fire: 600 rpm (cyclic)
Magazine: 25- or 32-round box
Users: police and military forces in at least 20 countries

Largely manufactured from cheap pressed steel, the Uzi is one of the most influential sub-machine gun designs of the post-war years.

Model 12 sub-machine gun

BERETTA SUB-MACHINE GUNS have always been superbly made, and were highly sought-after trophies in World War II. The **Model 12**, introduced in the late 1950s, was built to the same high standard, although for the first time stamped metal and plastic were used in the weapon's manufacture.

Like the Uzi, the Model 12 uses a wraparound bolt to reduce the overall length of the gun, but it is a more conventional design, with the magazine housing ahead of the pistol grip. It was equipped with both a grip safety, which had to be held down to allow the action to be cocked, and a push-button safety above the pistol grip. It was available with a fixed wooden stock or a folding metal stock.

Externally, the improved **Model 12S** looks very similar to its predecessor, but incorporates a number of detail improvements. It now has a single lever safety and fire selector, above the trigger, which can be operated by the right thumb. The firer can select 'S' for safe, 'I' for semi-automatic or single-shot fire, and 'R' for full-auto fire. The sights have been improved and strengthened, It also comes with a hard-wearing epoxy resin surface, increasing resistance to corrosion and wear.

The Model 12 has been issued to Italian special operations units, and is a popular choice with protection and hostage rescue units around the world. It has been sold to many countries in North Africa, Latin America and the Far East.

Manufactured to the Beretta company's customary high standard, in skilled hands the Model 12 is capable of shooting with considerable accuracy.

SPECIFICATION

Name: Model 12S
Type: sub-machine gun
Calibre: 9-mm x 19 Parabellum
Weight: empty 3.2 kg
Dimensions: length 660 mm, stock extended; barrel length 260 mm
Muzzle velocity: 380 metres per second
Effective range: 200 m
Rate of fire: 500-550 rpm (cyclic)
Magazine: 20-, 32- or 40-round box
Users: Italy, Brazil, Gabon, Indonesia, Libya, Nigeria, Saudi Arabia, Tunisia, Venezuela

A dramatic break with pre-war Beretta designs, the Model 12 makes use of heavy sheet metal stampings for ease of manufacture.

ITALY
Spectre sub-machine gun

URBAN TERRORISM HAS BEEN a significant factor in Italian life for many years, and the Spectre has been developed specifically for counter-terrorism and unconventional warfare.

Announced in 1983, the **Spectre** has a number of features which suit it to the task. It has a unique four-column 50-round magazine, which takes up less room than a 30-round magazine of more conventional double-column design. The Spectre appears conventional, if a little futuristic. But unlike other compact sub-machine guns, it fires from a closed bolt, making it highly accurate.

It is a double-action gun; it can be carried cocked with a round chambered, but with the hammer disengaged. Pulling the trigger engages the hammer rather like in a double-action revolver. Carrying the

The Spectre's thick four-column magazine ensures that any user of the sub-machine gun has plenty of firepower at his disposal.

weapon this way means that you do not have to spend valuable moments looking for the bolt cocking your weapon if you are ambushed by terrorists.

Small and handy but with devastating firepower, the Spectre is a superb personal protection weapon.

SPECIFICATION
Name: Spectre
Type: sub-machine gun
Calibre: 9-mm x 19 Parabellum
Weight: empty 2.9 kg
Dimensions: length 350 mm, stock retracted ; barrel length 130 mm
Muzzle velocity: 400 m/sec
Effective range: 150 m
Rate of fire: 850 rpm (cyclic)
Magazine: 30- or 50- round box
Users: various undisclosed police and military bodyguard units

The Spectre's two-handed grip and ease of use ensures instinctive, accurate shooting.

SWEDEN
Carl Gustav sub-machine gun

The Carl Gustav has been the Swedish army's standard sub-machine gun for over 40 years.

It remains in service with the Swedish army, which uses a special high-velocity 9-mm round which, it is claimed, has greater range and penetration than any other type of sub-machine gun ammunition.

Many post-war sub-machine gun designs were simple but built to a very high standard, and the Swedish Carl Gustav is no exception.

THE **KULSPRUTA PISTOL M/45** sub-machine gun is known as the **Carl Gustav**, after the Carl Gustavs Stads Gevärfactori, where it was manufactured for the Swedish army. Like many contemporary sub-machine guns of the 1940s and 1950s the Carl Gustav is a heavy weapon, solidly built from machined steel parts.

Its double-column magazine is noted for its reliability, and has been widely copied by other manufacturers. The Carl Gustav was used in Southeast Asia by US-supplied irregular troops and by US Army special forces, who developed a silenced variant for clandestine operations. Many Carl Gustavs were sold to Egypt, where the type was also put into production as the '**Port Said'**.

SPECIFICATION
Name: KP m/45 (Carl Gustav)
Type: sub-machine gun
Calibre: 9-mm Patron m/39 (9-mm x 19 Parabellum)
Weight: 3.9 kg empty
Dimensions: 808 mm stock extended; barrel length 213 mm
Muzzle velocity: 410 metres per second
Effective range: 220 m
Rate of fire: 600 rpm (cyclic)
Magazine: 36-round box
Users: Sweden, Egypt, Indonesia, Ireland

SPAIN
Z-84 sub-machine gun

Star weapons are manufactured in Spain's Basque country, one of Europe's great traditional gun-making regions.

the barrel as long as possible, hence maximising accuracy. It also has the Uzi-like feature of housing the magazine in the pistol grip.

There are no external moving parts; the cocking handle moves forward under spring power and remains still during firing. The **Z-84** is highly water-resistant, and it can handle hollow-point and semi-jacketed ammunition as well as standard military full-metal-jacket rounds. These features make it an effective weapon for security forces and marine assault troops as well as for commandos and special operations units.

FOR MANY YEARS AFTER World War II, the standard sub-machine gun of the Spanish army was the model **Z45** manufactured by the old-established Basque firm of Star, Bonifacio Echeverria. This was basically the German wartime MP-40 with minor improvements. It was succeeded by the **Z62**, a blowback design with a complex trigger, and the **Z-70/B** with a more conventional trigger.

In the 1980s, Star introduced the completely new **Star Model Z-84**. Like many modern sub-machine guns, the Z-84 looks very like the Uzi. It is more than a Uzi clone, however, although like the highly influential Israeli weapon it makes extensive use of steel stampings and has a similar wrap-around bolt. This cuts overall length while keeping

SPECIFICATION
Name: Z-84
Type: sub-machine gun
Calibre: 9-mm x 19 Parabellum
Weight: 3 kg empty
Dimensions: 808 mm, stock extended; barrel length 213 mm
Muzzle velocity: 410 metres per second
Effective range: 220 m
Rate of fire: 600 rpm (cyclic)
Magazine: 36-round box
User: Spain

L2A3 Sterling sub-machine gun

THE **STERLING** HAS BEEN the British Army's standard sub-machine gun since the 1950s. Designated the **L2**, the main production variant is the **L2A3**. It has armed radio operators, NCOs, weapons crews, drivers and other personnel for more than three decades, but it has been replaced in combat units by the SA80 Bullpup rifle.

Although the Sterling looks like a cheap pressed steel weapon, it is actually extremely solid, made mostly from machined parts. It does not use the wraparound bolt pioneered by the Czech CZ-25 and the Uzi. Although the Sterling is longer than the Uzi, its barrel is more than six centimetres shorter.

The high-quality construction means that the

British troops have used the Sterling since the 1950s. The solidly-made gun has proved accurate and reliable in climates as varied as Norway's Arctic winter and the searing heat of Arabia.

Sterling is extremely reliable, and performs well in the most adverse of conditions. Although expensive, it is nevertheless one of the world's most widely used sub-machine guns.

SPECIFICATION

Name: L2A3
Type: sub-machine gun
Calibre: 9-mm x 19 Parabellum
Weight: 2.72 kg empty
Dimensions: 690 mm, stock extended; barrel length 198 mm
Muzzle velocity: 390 m/sec
Effective range: 200 m
Rate of fire: 550 rpm (cyclic)
Magazine: 10-, 15-, or 34-round box
Users: UK and more than 90 other countries

The Sterling bears a resemblance to its predecessor, the cheap and effective Sten gun. But the Sterling is a far more solidly manufactured weapon, reliable under all conditions.

The Sterling is instantly recognisable thanks to its side-mounted magazine, a feature rare today although common in the first generation of SMGs.

USA
M1 Thompson sub-machine gun

In spite of their heavy weight, Thompsons were favoured weapons for airborne troops in WWII.

Vietnam War, the Thompson would have been obsolete but for the collapse of Yugoslavia. Large numbers of these elderly sub-machine guns were still in Yugoslav arsenals in 1991, and they are now back in the front line.

THE **THOMPSON** BECAME FAMOUS, or notorious, as the 'gangster gun' of the 1920s and 1930s. Later, as the **M1928** or the **M1A1**, chambered for the .45 ACP cartridge, it was widely used during World War II by American and Allied forces.

Very heavy and solidly constructed, the 'Tommy Gun' is a handsome and robust weapon. Its high standard of manufacture is a testimony to the craftsmanship of a bygone era, which would be prohibitively expensive today.

Although used in combat until the end of the

Although long obsolete, the heavy Thompson gun will be around for many years to come in the hands of guerrillas.

SPECIFICATION
Name: M1A1
Type: sub-machine gun
Calibre: .45 ACP
Weight: 4.82 kg empty
Dimensions: length 813 mm; barrel length 266 mm
Muzzle velocity: 277 metres per second
Effective range: 150 m
Rate of fire: 700 rpm (cyclic)
Magazine: 20- or 30-round box
Users: militia, irregulars and guerrillas all over the world

USA
M3 sub-machine gun

Although the 'Grease Gun' was never as popular as the Thompson, it was an effective weapon which cost much less to make than its predecessor.

M3A1s manufactured. In the 1950s and 1960s many other countries manufactured M3s under licence or produced all but identical copies.

The M3 remained a standard US Army weapon well into the post-war years, and was still in regular front-line service in 1960. Although superseded in infantry hands by the development of the full-auto capable assault rifle, the M3 could still be found with tank crews and other soldiers operating in enclosed spaces in 1980.

M3s may still be found in reserve or in service with irregular units and guerrilla forces in South America and Southeast Asia.

Designed like the British Sten gun for rapid, low-cost manufacture, the **M3** was a functional but ugly weapon. It was christened the **'Grease Gun'** because it looked more at home in a mechanic's tool box than a soldier's kit

It was simple, robust, and had a very low rate of fire to help soldiers control the bucking recoil of the .45 cartridge, but it was never regarded with the same affection as the Thompson. Much of this could be traced to the unsatisfactory magazine, which was sensitive to dirt and rough handling and gave constant feed troubles through its service life.

Simple though it was, the M3 could be made even more basic. The **M3A1** of 1944 eliminated the bolt retraction mechanism, the weapon being cocked by the firer inserting a finger into a recess in the bolt and pulling.

By 1944, General Motors was turning out M3s at a rate of 8,000 per week. Production ceased at the end of the war with 650,000 M3s and over 700,000

SPECIFICATION
Name: M3A1
Type: sub-machine gun
Calibre: .45 ACP
Weight: 3.47 kg empty
Dimensions: length 757 mm; barrel length 266 mm
Muzzle velocity: 280 metres per second
Effective range: 150 m
Rate of fire: 450 rpm (cyclic)
Magazine: 30-round box
Users: reserves, irregulars and guerrillas

Ingram Model 10 sub-machine gun

The Ingram Model 11 (left) is a smaller, handier version of the Model 10 (left below). This example is fitted with a suppressor, which is covered in heat-resistant Nomex.

THANKS TO HOLLYWOOD, the **Ingram Model 10** is one of the world's best-known small arms. The boxy little gun with the high rate of fire is the favoured weapon of celluloid drug dealers and undercover cops.

But the Ingram is more than a film prop. Designed by Gordon B. Ingram, the Model 10 is a robust little gun available in .45 ACP or 9-mm Parabellum. The high rate of fire can spray out a lot of bullets, but makes the weapon very difficult to control. The **Model 11**, a smaller version of the gun chambered for the less powerful 9-mm Short round, is easier to handle.

The muzzle on most Ingrams is threaded for a suppressor, and when this is fitted it is usually covered with heat-resistant material and can be used as a foregrip, which is much more effective than the strap normally provided and is a great aid to accuracy.

The Ingram has had a chequered manufacturing history, having been built by several companies. These have included the Military Armaments Corporation of Georgia, whose initials gave rise to the **MAC 10** name by which the weapon is often known.

The Model 11 has most recently been manufactured by SWD Inc. as the **Cobray M11**.

SPECIFICATION

Name: Ingram Model 10
Type: sub-machine gun
Calibre: .45 ACP or 9-mm x 19 Parabellum
Weight: 2.84 kg empty
Dimensions: 548 mm, stock extended; barrel length 213 mm
Muzzle velocity: 280 metres per second
Effective range: 100 m
Rate of fire: 1145 rpm (cyclic)
Magazine: 16- or 32-round box
Users: Bolivia, Colombia, Guatemala, Honduras, Israel, Portugal, UK, USA, Venezuela, and wide commercial sales

---

AC-556F sub-machine gun

Developed from the Ruger Mini-14 rifle, the AC-556F is one of the most powerful sub-machine gun type weapons currently available.

THE LINE BETWEEN ASSAULT RIFLES and sub-machine guns has become increasingly blurred. Originally designed to incorporate lessons from the trench fighting of World War I, the sub-machine gun was essentially a short-range weapon for use in enclosed spaces, designed to pump out a high volume of fire. To ease controllability, the weapons were chambered to fire low-power pistol rounds.

The assault rifle evolved during World War II to increase the firepower available to the infantryman. Like the sub-machine gun, it is capable of fully automatic fire. However, full-power rifle rounds are all but impossible to control in a hand-held weapon, so a new class of cartridge of intermediate power was developed. These have since been replaced by rifles designed to fire small-calibre high-velocity rounds.

The Ruger Mini-14 is a well-known 5.56-mm calibre assault rifle, based on the well-tried mechanicals of the M1 and M14 full-power battle rifles, which is available in both semi-automatic and selective fire versions. The full-auto variant is the **AC-556**.

There is a carbine version of the AC-556, known as the **AC-556F**, which has folding stock and a shortened barrel. Handy and easy to fire, it is designed for operation in enclosed spaces, and shares many of the characteristics of the sub-machine gun. However, it is still longer than most sub-machine guns, and while the 5.56 x 45-mm rounds it fires is of smaller calibre it has three times the muzzle velocity of 9-mm Parabellum. This means that the **AC-556** is more accurate and has a considerably longer range than similar-sized weapons firing pistol cartridges.

SPECIFICATION

Name: AC-556F
Type: sub-machine gun
Calibre: 5.56-mm x 45 NATO
Weight: 3.27 kg empty
Dimensions: 584 mm, stock folded; barrel length 292 mm
Muzzle velocity: 1000 metres per second
Effective range: 350 m
Rate of fire: 750 rpm (cyclic)
Magazine: 20- or 30-round box
Users: military and security forces in the USA and worldwide

USSR
PPSh-41 sub-machine gun

The PPSh-41 was made by the million during World War II, and was used for years afterwards.

Mosin-Nagant rifle barrels in half! The PPSh had two types of magazine: a conventional single-stack 35-round box or a giant drum magazine capable of holding 71 rounds.

Crudely built, but extremely tough and reliable, the PPSh-41 can still be found in use in odd parts of the world.

ONE OF THE MOST FAMOUS weapons used in World War II, the **PPSh-41** was subsequently copied in China and became the main Communist infantry weapon in the Korean War. Remaining in reserve formations throughout the Warsaw Pact well into the 1960s, it was still being used in Beirut during the 1980s and also in Africa.

With light recoil and reasonable accuracy at up to 150 metres, the PPSh-41 was extremely robust. The barrels were chrome-lined to offer some protection against the corrosive primers used on Soviet ammunition, although when demand was at its height many PPSh barrels were made by cutting

SPECIFICATION
Name: PPSh-41
Type: sub-machine gun
Calibre: 7.62-mm x 25
Weight: 3.64 kg empty
Dimensions: 838 mm; barrel length 266 mm
Muzzle velocity: 488 metres per second
Effective range: 150 m
Rate of fire: 900 rpm (cyclic)
Magazine: 35- round box or 71- round drum
Users: rebel groups in Angola, Ethiopia, Lebanon, Somalia and others

USSR
PPS-43 sub-machine gun

Tough, reliable and simple to manufacture, the PPS-43 can still be found all over the world.

Soviet clients and allies. It was also manufactured in China, and is still used by second-line units in many countries.

SPECIFICATION
Name: PPS-43
Type: sub-machine gun
Calibre: 7.62-mm x 25
Weight: 3.36 kg empty
Dimensions: 820 mm; barrel length 272 mm
Muzzle velocity: 490 metres per second
Effective range: 150 m
Rate of fire: 700 rpm (cyclic)
Magazine: 35-round box
Users: some irregular forces

The PPS is about as simple a weapon as you can get, but it is easy and cheap to manufacture, and it works under all conditions.

THE **PPS-43** IS A REMARKABLE example of Soviet ingenuity. It was designed by engineer A.I. Sudarev in the besieged city of Leningrad (St Petersburg) in 1942, when it was encircled by German and Finnish forces and was desperately short of weapons.

Sudarev fashioned a very basic SMG from sheet metal stampings, held together by welds and rivets. Using the same stick magazine as existing Soviet SMGs and chambered for the same 7.62-mm x 25 pistol round, the PPS was built in Leningrad and used by the city's garrison.

It proved a sturdy and reliable weapon, and after the siege was lifted in 1943 production standards improved and the resulting PPS-43 was supplied to other Soviet units, and was widely distributed to

ASSAULT RIFLES

AUSTRIA
AUG assault rifle

IN SPITE OF ITS SPACE-AGE appearance, the **Armee Universal Gewehr (AUG)** manufactured by Steyr has been in service for nearly two decades. The first of the modern 'bullpup' rifles, the AUG has won an enviable reputation for toughness

Much of its success derives from the fact that it is a small-arms system. Barrels, working parts and magazine housings are interchangeable, allowing the AUG to become anything from a sub-machine gun or para rifle to a heavy-barrelled sniper's rifle or light machine-gun.

The weapon is extremely strong: in tests an AUG has stayed in working order after repeatedly being run over by a 10-tonne truck. Its transparent

The AUG's combination of accuracy and reliability has seen it adopted by armies around the world, from Ireland (above) to its native Austria (below).

plastic magazine lets the firer know at a glance just how many rounds he has left. It is also highly damage-resistant, unlike the metal magazines of other 5.56-mm rifles.

The AUG is the standard rifle of the Austrian army, where it is known as the Sturmgewehr 77, and it is also used by armies and law enforcement agencies around the world.

SPECIFICATION
Name: AUG
Type: assault rifle
Calibre: 5.56-mm x 45 NATO
Weight: empty 3.6 kg
Dimensions: length 790 mm; barrel length 508 mm
Muzzle velocity: 980 m/sec
Effective range: 400 m
Rate of fire: 650 rpm (cyclic)
Magazine: 30- or 42-round box
Users: Austria, Australia, Eire, Oman, Saudi Arabia, US Customs service, many others

The AUG was one of the first infantry weapons to offer an optical sight as standard.

The AUG's x1.4 sight has been optimised for battlefield ranges. It can be replaced by a mount for other telescopic and night vision sights.

FAL battle rifle

THE **FUSIL AUTOMATIQUE LÉGÈRE** or **FAL**, manufactured by Fabrique National, was originally designed to fire the 7.92-mm *kurz* cartridge developed by the Germans in World War II. However, post-war US pressure for a more powerful cartridge produced the compromise 7.62-mm x 51, which could be easily manufactured on machines then producing the American .30 calibre service cartridge. The new, more powerful round was selected as the NATO standard.

FN rebuilt their rifle to fit the new cartridge and created what is possibly the classic post-war battle rifle. Tough, reliable, and accurate, the new design promptly cornered the market, selling to armed

Dutch Marines train in the Arctic. The lead soldier is equipped with a heavy-barrelled FAL, suitable for use as a light machine-gun.

forces in dozens of countries around the world.

The British Army used it until the late 1980s, and some remain in service with reserve and support units. British and Australian FNs were modified to prevent fully automatic fire, which is almost impossible to control.

All FALs share the reliability that solid construction and attention to detail creates. Most are also capable of automatic fire.

SPECIFICATION

Name: FAL
Type: battle rifle
Calibre: 7.62-mm x 51 NATO
Weight: empty 4.325 kg
Dimensions: length 1090 mm; barrel length 533 mm
Muzzle velocity: 840 metres per second
Effective range: 650 m
Rate of fire: 650-700 rpm (cyclic)
Magazine: 20-round box
Users: more than 90 countries including Argentina, Australia, Belgium, Canada, India, Israel, Libya, Peru, Singapore, UK

Although the FAL has been produced in many variants, from short-barrel para versions with folding skeleton stocks to heavy-barrel support weapons, most have been versions of the basic battle rifle depicted here.

BELGIUM
FNC assault rifle

The FNC is a capable 5.56-mm calibre rifle, which has achieved some success, although nowhere near that of the preceding FAL.

THE BELGIAN FIRM OF Fabrique National is well known for its 7.62-mm FN FAL rifle, which has proved itself in combat on countless occasions. It has been a world standard weapon since the 1950s, in use by more than 90 countries. However, the FAL is very much a weapon of its time. With the trend from the 1960s tending towards weapons firing smaller-calibre high-velocity rounds, the FAL was seen as being simply too powerful.

After a false start with the expensive **CAL**, resembling a scaled-down FAL, the **FNC** is Fabrique National's response to the trend towards smaller-calibre battlefield weapons. It is a lightweight 5.56-mm rifle originally intended for infantry operating without continuous logistic support, or who are in difficult terrain such as jungles or mountains. The FNC is gas-operated, with a piston cylinder above the barrel. It has been tested by many countries and has been adopted by at least seven armies, including those of Belgium and Sweden.

SPECIFICATION
Name: FNC
Type: assault rifle
Calibre: 5.56-mm x 45 NATO
Weight: empty 3.8 kg
Dimensions: length 997 mm; barrel length 449 mm
Muzzle velocity: 965 metres per second
Effective range: 350 m
Rate of fire: 625-750 rpm (cyclic)
Magazine: 30-round box
Users: Belgium, Indonesia, Nigeria, Tonga, Sweden, Zaire, others

The FNC is designed for prolonged use in harsh conditions with minimal maintenance.

BELGIUM
Modèle 49 battle rifle

The Modèle 49 was a competent design which inspired the much better FAL.

THE RIFLE WHICH BECAME known as the **Fusil Automatique Modèle 49** dates back to the beginning of World War II. Designer Dieudonné Saive of Fabrique National d'Armes de Guerre fled to England and spent the war working on small-arms design for the British, to whom he offered his new rifle. When it was rejected by the British Army he returned to Belgium, and it was placed in production by his old company after the war

Known variously as the **Saive Automatique FN**, **SAFN**, **Saive**, **Arme Belgique Légère** or **ABL**, the weapon is gas-operated. Gas tapped from the top of the barrel acts on a long cylinder which in turn drives back the bolt. Cams in the side of the receiver tilt and lock the bolt, in a very strong action which can withstand a great deal of very hard use. The action was carefully machined out of high-quality materials, which contributed to the rifle's durability but added greatly to its cost.

The post-war market for self-loading rifles was surprisingly active, and Fabrique National offered the Modèle 49 in a variety of calibres, including 7-mm and 7.65-mm favoured in Europe, the American .30-inch (7.62-mm), and the the German 7.92-mm then widely used on Mauser-type rifles. All versions had 10-round magazines which could be loaded by charger or with individual rounds. The rifle was offered in standard (self-loading), selective fire, automatic only and sniper versions.

The Modèle 49 made Fabrique National a great deal of money, large orders being placed by a number of countries in South America, North Africa and Southeast Asia. It may still be encountered in Egypt or South America. However, the Saive design's major claim to fame was that it was the starting point for the team which developed FN's classic Fusil Automatique Légère, the FN FAL.

SPECIFICATION
Name: Modèle 49
Type: assault rifle
Calibre: 7-mm, 7.65-mm, 7.92-mm and .30-inch
Weight: empty 4.31 kg
Dimensions: length 1116 mm; barrel length 590 mm
Muzzle velocity: c. 730 m/sec (depending on calibre)
Effective range: 650 m
Rate of fire: 625-750 rpm (cyclic)
Magazine: 10-round box
Users: Colombia, Egypt, Indonesia, Venezuela

CZECHOSLOVAKIA
vz 52 battle rifle

The vz 52 was one of the few modern automatic rifle types to have been issued with a permanently-attached bayonet.

FOR MANY YEARS THE CZECH armaments industry in Brno was one of the most advanced in the world. In the 1920s, a team led by Emmanuel Holek produced a gas-piston-operated assault rifle called the **ZH 29** which was extensively tested by armies around the world. Reliable but heavy, few examples found their way into military service, but they did inspire the classic ZB series of light machine-guns which were to lead to the Bren gun.

The **ZK 420** which followed was a wartime design. This was an extremely well-made weapon, but offered little more than the huge quantity of new and surplus designs which flooded the world markets in the years after 1945.

The ZK 420's failure was in part due to the Czech army's adoption of the **Samonabiject Puska vz 52**. This was a not particularly inspired self-loading rifle developed in Czechoslovakia in the brief interlude between German and Soviet occupation. Its operation was largely cribbed from the MKb42(W), a Walther-designed wartime German assault rifle, and

the trigger was copied from the M1 Garand. Chambered for the Czech 7.62-mm round, some rifles designated **vz 52/57** were modified to fire Soviet 7.62-mm x 39 after the Czech forces were incorporated into the Warsaw Pact.

The Czech army dropped the vz 52 as soon as supplies of the **vz 58** assault rifle began to arrive. This was a robust and smooth-acting weapon, bearing an external resemblance to the Soviet Kalashnikov but employing a different bolt and hammer and a simplified trigger mechanism.

SPECIFICATION
Name: vz 52
Type: battle rifle
Calibre: 7.62-mm x 45 Czech or 7.62-mm x 39 Soviet
Weight: empty 4.08 kg
Dimensions: length 1015 mm; barrel length 520 mm
Muzzle velocity: 750 metres per second
Effective range: 500 m
Rate of fire: single-shot semi-auto only
Magazine: 1-round box
Users: Czechoslovakia; now obsolete but may be found in reserve

---

FINLAND
Valmet M76 assault rifle

Valmet rifles differ from the AK in appearance and finish, but mechanically they are modernised and improved versions of the Soviet rifle.

SANDWICHED BETWEEN East and West for much of the Cold War, and with a long border with the Soviet Union, Finland was one of the few countries able to select armaments from both sides of the Iron Curtain.

The Finns adopted the Kalashnikov design in the late 1950s, and a small batch of rifles was manufactured by the Sako concern as the **M60 Valmet**. With slight modifications, the type was put into full-scale production as the **M62**. Furniture was plastic rather than wood, and an aperture rear sight was fitted in place of the Soviet leaf sight.

By the 1970s the weapon had evolved into the much improved **M76**, which was also available with

a tubular folding buttstock. The Valmet rifles have been manufactured in both 5.56-mm NATO and 7.62-mm Soviet calibres.

The M76 has been supplemented by the new **M90**, which still shows its Kalashnikov ancestry but which has been made lighter and considerably more refined. The FAL-like folding stock gives it a similar appearance to the Israeli Galil, in itself a development of the influential Soviet design.

As with the earlier rifles, the M90 is available in either 5.56-mm or 7.62-mm Soviet calibres. Sako have developed a new alloy bullet for the weapon, capable of penetrating more than 15 mm of steel.

SPECIFICATION
Name: Valmet M76
Type: assault rifle
Calibre: 7.62-mm x 39 Soviet or 5.56-mm x 45 NATO
Weight: empty 3.6 kg
Dimensions: length 950 mm; barrel length 418 mm
Muzzle velocity: 720/960 metres per second
Effective range: 300-400 m
Rate of fire: 600-750 rpm cyclic
Magazine: 15-, 20-, or 30-round box
Users: Finland, Indonesia, Qatar

FRANCE
MAS 49/56 battle rifle

THE FRENCH ARMY WAS THE LAST to develop a bolt-action service rifle: the MAS 36, fielded in the 1930s. But wartime experience showed that they needed a self-loader. The **MAS 49**, produced by Manufacture d'Armes de Saint-Etienne, was the result. It was a new weapon, although it used the butt, stock and sights of the old rifle.

Rather heavy for its size, the gas-operated MAS 49 was modified in the mid-1950s as the **MAS 49/56**, with a shorter stock and a new flash-hider/grenade-launcher, the first rifle to have such a device permanently attached.

Tough and reliable, the MAS 49 served the French army very well in Indo-China and Algeria, and was not replaced until the 1980s. The only drawback for non-French forces is the use of the French 7.5-mm cartridge, but some have been produced in 7.62-mm NATO.

SPECIFICATION
Name: MAS 49/56
Type: battle rifle
Calibre: 7.5-mm x 54
Weight: empty 3.9 kg
Dimensions: length 1010 mm; barrel length 521 mm
Muzzle velocity: 810 metres per second
Effective range: 600 m
Rate of fire: single-shot semi-auto only
Magazine: 10-round box
Users: France, mostly in reserve; widely used in former French colonies

The MAS 49 was one of the first rifles to be fitted with an integral grenade-launcher/flash hider.

FRANCE
FA MAS assault rifle

One of the most compact rifles now in service, the FA MAS has a very high rate of fire.

FRENCH 20TH-CENTURY small-arms design has generally lagged well behind the rest of the world, but with the **FA MAS** assault rifle it made up ground with a vengeance. It is an example of the overall compactness which can be achieved by using a 'bullpup' configuration, with the magazine and breech located behind the trigger group. The FA MAS takes the concept to extremes, being even shorter than contemporary designs like the British SA80 and the Austrian AUG.

Despite its unusual appearance, giving rise to its French nickname of '*Le Clarion*' (the bugle), the FA MAS is relatively easy to handle and fire. The fire selector offers single-shot, three-round burst and full automatic. It fires the NATO standard 5.56-mm round, but has a very high rate of fire and needs a delicate finger on the trigger when firing automatically to avoid wasting ammunition.

The long carrying handle over the top of the receiver doubles as a base for the fore and rear sights, and gives them a certain amount of protection against rough handling. There is provision for a small bayonet, and folding bipod legs are fitted as standard. As with the preceding MAS 49, there is a permanently attached grenade-launching mount at the short protruding muzzle. As with all bullpups, it has a tactical drawback in that without modification it cannot be fired left-handed.

The FA MAS has proved to be an effective assault rifle in service, although its trigger pull is not all that could be desired and requires practice to master. Introduced to action in the early 1980s in Lebanon and Chad, it has since seen extensive service in the Gulf War and in Bosnia.

SPECIFICATION
Name: FA MAS
Type: assault rifle
Calibre: 5.56-mm x 45 NATO
Weight: empty 3.61 kg
Dimensions: length 757 mm; barrel length 488 mm
Muzzle velocity: 960 metres per second
Effective range: 300 m
Rate of fire: 900-1000 rpm (cyclic)
Magazine: 25-round box
Users: France, Djibouti, Gabon, Senegal, UAE

G3 battle rifle

THE HECKLER & KOCH **G3** is one of the world's most widely used battle rifles. Developed in the 1950s, it was first issued to the Bundeswehr in 1959 and has been the German army's service rifle since then.

The G3 works by delayed blowback, like a pistol or sub-machine gun rather than firing from a locked breech like most rifles and machine-guns. It uses the roller-locking system originating in the Mauser Sturmgewehr StG 45 during World War II, and developed by Mauser engineers who had moved to Spain after the war. The design was acquired and improved by Heckler & Koch, which has applied the

The Heckler & Koch G3 has proved its reliability under combat conditions all over the world. Immensely strong and accurate, it is in service in more than 50 countries.

perfected roller locking system to most of the H&K range.

Slightly heavier than the contemporary FN FAL and with the cocking lever in a rather awkward position, the G3's accuracy and overall performance is similar to that of the Belgian rifle. With a few notable exceptions, the G3 has been adopted everywhere the FN FAL missed, equipping some 50 armies and being made under licence in at least 12 countries. Like the FN, the G3 design has been modified for 5.56-mm weapons, but these have not prospered like their larger predecessors.

The G3 has proved to be dependable in the freezing ice and snow of Norway's Arctic wilderness.

The G3 is made largely from sheet metal stampings with plastic furniture, requiring a minimum of expensive machining to complete.

SPECIFICATION

Name: G3
Type: battle rifle
Calibre: 7.62-mm x 51 NATO
Weight: empty 4.4 kg
Dimensions: length 1025 mm; barrel length 450 mm
Muzzle velocity: 780-800 metres per second
Effective range: 500 m
Rate of fire: 500-600 rpm (cyclic)
Magazine: 20-round box
Users: Germany and more than 50 countries around the world. The G3 is licence-manufactured in France, Greece, Norway, Portugal, Sweden, Turkey, UK, Mexico, Sudan, Tanzania, Togo, Uganda and Zambia

H&K 5.56-mm assault rifle

THE G3 RIFLE MANUFACTURED by the German firm of Heckler & Koch is one of the classic post-war small-arms designs. Used extensively around the world, its operating system has formed the basis for many other products from Heckler & Koch.

The almost bewildering variety of weapons which use the H&K roller locking system covers everything from sub-machine .guns through rifles and sniper rifles to medium machine-guns. Naturally, the family of weapons also includes several examples of modern small-calibre assault rifles.

The **HK33** is a top-of-the-line 5.56-mm calibre assault rifle which is scaled down from the full-power G3 rifle and uses the same well-proven firing mechanism and trigger. It is available in full-length and shortened carbine versions, and comes with the usual Heckler & Koch range of options including fixed and sliding butts, bipod and telescopic or iron sights. The weapon is well manufactured, and it shoots and handles well. The HK33 has achieved a considerable degree of export success in Asia, Africa and South America.

The **HK53** straddles the line between sub-

All H&K weapons have similar controls. If you know where the safety and fire selector is on one weapon, you can find it on the HK33 or the G41.

Using the same basic layout as the best-selling G3 rifle, the HK33 exists in several versions, including sniper and reduced-size carbine models.

machine-guns and rifles. Basically a drastically cut-down HK33, it is very like the MP5 SMG in size but is far more powerful since it is chambered for the the 5.56-mm NATO rifle cartridge.

The latest of the H&K 5.56 mm weapons is the **G41**. Similar to the HK33, it has been optimised to fire the current NATO standard SS109 round and can give single-shot, three-round burst or fully automatic fire. It has a low-noise bolt closing device, a bolt catch which keeps the bolt open when all rounds have been fired, and the cartridge ejection port has a dustproof cover. The G41 can accept any M16-type magazine, and has a built-in mount for NATO standard night and telescopic sights. A bipod can be fitted, and it can accept G3 bayonets.

SPECIFICATION

Name: HK33E
Type: assault rifle
Calibre: 5.56-mm x 45 NATO
Weight: empty 3.65 kg
Dimensions: length 920 mm; barrel length 390 mm
Muzzle velocity: 920 metres per second
Effective range: 400 m
Rate of fire: 750 rpm (cyclic)
Magazine: 25-round box
Users: Brazil, Chile, Malaysia, Thailand and other countries in Africa, South America and Asia

Name: G41
Weight: empty 4.1 kg
Dimensions: length 997 mm; barrel length 450 mm
Muzzle velocity: 920 metres per second
Effective range: 400 m
Rate of fire: 850 rpm (cyclic)
Magazine: 30-round box
Users: Germany; under evaluation by a number of armies and security forces

Galil assault rifle

THE **GALIL** RIFLE IS ONE OF the most battle-worthy small arms in the world, born as it was out of more than four decades of struggle between Israel and her Arab neighbours.

With almost every Arab opponent armed with the AK-47, the Israeli Defence Force has unrivalled experience of the Soviet weapon's strengths and weaknesses. The Israelis noted the exceptional sturdiness and reliability of the AK as well as its simplicity – it does not take long to teach someone to shoot and maintain a Kalashnikov.

Israel developed the Galil rifle along very similar lines. It uses the basic Kalashnikov action, but more care in manufacture and the use of better raw materials have led to improved accuracy.

Available in 5.56 mm or 7.62 mm and in a choice of barrel lengths, the Galil has appeared in a number of versions. The **Galil ARM** is equipped with a bipod which doubles as a wire cutter and is

The Galil is a classic Israeli weapon. Take a captured rifle like the AK-47, put it into production but with improvements, and you emerge with one of the most combat-ready rifles in the world.

designed to be used as a rifle or light machine-gun. The **Galil AR**, equipped with a folding metal stock but no bipod, is the assault rifle variant. A shortened version for use from more confined spaces is known as the **Galil SAR**. There is also a very accurate sniper version.

The Galil achieved some export success. It is made under licence in South Africa, whose R4 is even more strongly built than the original in order to withstand long operations in the bush.

SPECIFICATION
Name: Galil ARM 5.56
Type: assault rifle
Calibre: 5.56-mm x 45 or 7.62-mm x 51 NATO
Weight: empty 4.35 kg
Dimensions: length 979 mm; barrel length 460 mm
Muzzle velocity: 950 metres per second
Effective range: 500 m
Rate of fire: 650 rpm (cyclic)
Magazine: 35- or 50-round box
Users: Israeli defence forces, South Africa, some unspecified armies and police forces

Galils come in three main types: the Galil ARM with bipod and carrying handle, the Galil AR depicted here without either, and the short-barrelled SAR.

The Galil is available as the full-powered battle rifle seen here, firing 7.62-mm NATO rounds, or as an advanced assault rifle in 5.56-mm calibre.

ITALY
AR70 assault rifle

Beretta's AR70 is designed for use under the harshest of conditions, and has proved very successful as a jungle rifle.

but also takes in ideas and suggestions from military users of the AR70. As with most modern assault rifles, its magazine housing is compatible with M16-type magazines.

THE **AR70** WAS DEVELOPED by the Italian firm of Beretta in the 1970s after a careful study of existing small-calibre combat rifles. It is a straightforward 5.56-mm assault rifle with few frills, carefully designed to minimise the amount of dirt that can enter the weapon.

The AR70 is exceptionally easy to strip and maintain. Capable of automatic fire, its only problem is that the cocking handle is the only part connecting gas piston to bolt carrier: lose the handle and the weapon is unusable.

The Beretta 70/90 is an improved version developed for the Italian army. It incorporates the latest features such as a three-round burst facility,

SPECIFICATION
Name: AR70/90
Type: assault rifle
Calibre: 5.56-mm x 45 NATO
Weight: empty 3.99 kg
Dimensions: length 998 mm; barrel length 450 mm
Muzzle velocity: c. 950 metres per second
Effective range: 500 m
Rate of fire: 650 rpm (cyclic)
Magazine: 30-round box
Users: several armies including Italy, Jordan, and Malaysia

The AR 70/90 is the latest variant of Beretta's assault rifle design.

ITALY
BM 59 battle rifle

The BM 59 is a modernised M1 Garand, roughly equivalent to the American M14.

BERETTA BEGAN MAKING Garand rifles for the Italian army soon after World War II, and by 1961 some 100,000 examples had been completed. However, the introduction of NATO's new standard 7.62-mm round in the 1950s meant that these would have to be replaced as they fired the older American .30-in round.

Beretta's designers had for some time been contemplating a revision of the basic Garand design, to give selective-fire capability with as few mechanical changes as possible. In 1959 they introduced the Beretta **BM 59**, which was an M1 Garand at heart but was modified to take a 20-round magazine and able to fire the new 7.62-mm x 51 NATO cartridge fully automatically.

Variants began to appear soon after the new rifle was placed in production for the Italian armed forces. The **BM 59R** had a lower rate of fire, the **BM 59D** was equipped with a pistol grip and bipod, the **BM 59GL** had a grenade-launcher and the **BM 60CB** had a three-round burst fire adapter. These were later redesignated, the basic rifle being known as

the **Mk 1**. The Italian army version with light bipod is the **Mk Ital**. The **Mk II** has a pistol grip enlarged trigger guard for winter use and a bipod, while the **Mk III** has a folding metal stock. Cut-down Italian army versions of the Mk III for alpine and airborne use are known as the **Mk Ital TA** and the **Mk Ital Para**. The **Mk IV** is a heavy-barrelled version for use as a squad automatic weapon.

The BM 59 is an extremely robust and reliable rifle which has been a very effective and successful weapon. It is still in service with Italian forces, even though for front-line use it has been superseded by more modern assault rifles.

SPECIFICATION
Name: BM 59
Type: battle rifle
Calibre: 7.62-mm x 51 NATO
Weight: 4.6 kg
Dimensions: length 1095 mm; barrel length 490 mm
Muzzle velocity: c. 825 metres per second
Effective range: 600 m
Rate of fire: 750 rpm (cyclic)
Magazine: 20-round box
Users: Italy; also manufactured under licence in Indonesia and Morocco

SINGAPORE
SAR 80 assault rifle

The SAR 80 is a lightly-built modern assault rifle available with a full range of accessories.

gas-piston assault rifle with an attractive price tag.

Chartered Firearms Industries also produces the **SR88**, a lightweight gas-operated assault rifle using a rotating bolt. It has a chrome-plated gas piston system which almost eliminates carbon fouling.

THE RAPIDLY DEVELOPING island state of Singapore has one of the most advanced industrial capabilities in Asia. That industry is making a play for exports in a number of markets, one of which is in the field of small arms.

The **SAR 80** is produced by Chartered Industries of Singapore, the firearms division of which was founded in 1967 to manufacture the M16 under licence. Designed with the help of the British company Sterling, the SAR 80 is at least as effective as the American rifle, but is cheaper to build using the latest production techniques. The result is a basic,

SPECIFICATION
Name: SAR 80
Type: assault rifle
Calibre: 5.56-mm x 45 NATO
Weight: empty 3.7 kg
Dimensions: length 970 mm; barrel length 459 mm
Muzzle velocity: 970 metres per second
Effective range: 400 m
Rate of fire: 600-800 rpm (cyclic)
Magazine: 20- or 30-round box
Users: Singapore

The SAR has a manually controlled gas regulator which can be shut off when firing grenades.

SOUTH AFRICA
R-4 assault rifle

The R4 is a strengthened, enlarged version of the Israeli Galil ARM.

even more robust than the Israeli original. It also has a longer butt to suit the larger-statured South African soldiers.

Generally issued with nylon furniture and a plastic 35-round magazine, the R-4 includes the popular beer-bottle opener on the integral bipod. The sights have tritium inserts for night firing, set to 200 metres, below which the R-4 has a basically flat trajectory.

The R-5 is a carbine version without the bipod, mechanically identical to the R-4 although lighter and with a much shorter barrel. It has been issued to the Air Force and Marines of the new South African National Defence Force (SANDF).

SOUTH AFRICA'S LONG ISOLATION during the apartheid regime meant that the country had to develop its own indigenous arms industry. Now that this isolation has ended, the country's tough and effective products are bound to be encountered with more frequency on world markets.

For many years the South African Defence Force and the Republic's police units were equipped with FN FALs and Heckler & Koch G3 rifles. In the 1980s, following the worldwide shift to smaller-calibre assault rifles, the South Africans re-equipped with new **R-4** and **R-5** 5.56-mm rifles.

The R-4 is a development of the Israeli Galil, which in itself is a modernised version of the classic Soviet-designed Kalashnikov. The SADF's long experience of fighting in the bush far from any support facilities meant that they demanded that their new rifle be extremely tough, and the R4 is

SPECIFICATION
Name: R-4
Type: assault rifle
Calibre: 5.56-mm x 45 NATO
Weight: empty 4.35 kg
Dimensions: length 979 mm; barrel length 460 mm
Muzzle velocity: 950 metres per second
Effective range: 500 m
Rate of fire: 650 rpm (cyclic)
Magazine: 35- or 50-round box
Users: South Africa

CETME Model 58 battle rifle

The CETME rifle was based on a late-war German design. It has been the Spanish army's service rifle since the late 1950s, and will continue to serve Spain into the next century.

THE **CETME** RIFLE WAS THE product of a team of German designers from Mauser who set up shop in Spain in the years following the end of World War II.

Originally intended to fire the reduced-power 7.92-mm *kurz* round, the first production CETME rifle, which appeared in 1958, fired a unique cartridge. It was the same size as the then new 7.62-mm NATO standard round but of lower power. The CETME was the first rifle to use the roller-locking system later taken up by Heckler & Koch. The **CETME C3** is the final model of the rifle, and can fire full-power NATO rounds as well as the reduced-power Spanish cartridge.

The original rifle was made from stampings and low-grade steel. Later versions of the CETME design have either a light tubular bipod or a wooden foregrip/handguard.

SPECIFICATION

Name: CETME Model C
Type: battle rifle
Calibre: 7.62-mm x 51 NATO
Weight: empty 4.2 kg
Dimensions: length 1015 mm; barrel length 450 mm
Muzzle velocity: 780 metres per second
Effective range: 600 m
Rate of fire: 550-650 rpm (cyclic)
Magazine: 20-round box
Users: Spain; also supplied to Denmark, Norway, Pakistan, Portugal, and Sweden

The CETME was an early assault rifle, originating in a late-war Mauser design.

CETME Model L assault rifle

The Model L assault is a 5.56-mm adaptation of the full-power CETME rifle.

LIKE MANY OTHER WEAPONS DESIGNERS, Compañia de Estudios Técnicos de Materiales Especiales (CETME) has adapted its basic 7.62-mm battle rifle design to create an assault rifle firing the smaller NATO 5.56-mm round.

The **CETME Model L** is a natural development of the full-size CETME Model C and uses the same delayed blowback roller-locking operating system which is also employed in most of Heckler & Koch's wide range of firearms.

As with many of its contemporaries, the Model L originally offered a three-round burst facility as well as single-shot and full-auto fire. However, this is no longer a standard feature, although it can be specified when ordering the weapon, since most shooters easily learn to regulate bursts by trigger pressure alone.

A carbine version is also available. The **Model LC**

short assault rifle has a cut-down barrel and a sliding telescopic stock. With an overall length of 665 mm (stock retracted), it is much more suitable for use by paratroopers and mechanised troops operating from armoured vehicles and helicopters.

Originally offered with 20-round magazines, the Model L will now accept standard M16-pattern magazines, which may be prone to damage but are cheap and available all over the world.

The Model L handles well, but there are some questions about the type's long-term durability and reliability. After less than a decade of service problems are appearing, and the Spanish army is looking into the possibility of a replacement.

SPECIFICATION

Name: CETME Model L
Type: assault rifle
Calibre: 5.56-mm x 45 NATO
Weight: empty 3.4 kg
Dimensions: length 925 mm; barrel length 400 mm
Muzzle velocity: 875 metres per second
Effective range: 450 m
Rate of fire: 600-750 rpm (cyclic)
Magazine: 12- or 30-round box
Users: Spanish special forces

SWITZERLAND
SG540 assault rifles

Designed to the usual high Swiss standard, the French-built SG540 has achieved considerable export success in Africa and South America.

MANUFACTURED UNDER LICENCE by Manhurin in France, the **SG540** series of rifles designed by the Swiss SIG company has been very widely exported to African nations, particularly those formerly ruled by France. It is also used by armed forces in Asia and South America.

There are three types: the **SG540** and **SG543** are chambered for the M193 5.56-mm cartridge, while the **SG542** fires the 7.62-mm x 51 NATO round. All are gas-operated weapons with a rotating bolt, and the gas pressure can be adjusted to overcome resistance from dirt or snow in the mechanism. The rifles can be fired single-shot, fully automatic or in three-round bursts. In the latter case they fire three rounds in 0.25 seconds.

The current Swiss service rifle is the similar but even more robust **SG550** or **Stgw 90**. It replaces the SIG 510 series which was developed in the 1950s.

The SG550 is as accurate as its full-power predecessor out to battle ranges of 300 metres, although it carries twice as many rounds and is a little lighter. Like the SG540 it has a three-round burst controller, and the trigger guard can be folded aside to allow a soldier wearing Arctic mittens to reach the trigger without difficulty.

SPECIFICATION
Name: SG540
Type: assault rifle
Calibre: 5.56-mm x 45 NATO
Weight: empty 3.26 kg
Dimensions: length 950 mm; barrel length 460 mm
Muzzle velocity: 980 metres per second
Effective range: 600 m
Rate of fire: 650-800 rpm (cyclic)
Magazine: 20- or 30-round box
Users: more than 20 countries including Bolivia, Djibouti, Ecuador, France, Indonesia, Ivory Coast, Lebanon, Nicaragua, Oman, and the Seychelles

---

UNITED KINGDOM
L1A1 SLR battle rifle

The L1A1 SLR has served British and Commonwealth armies well, from the jungles of Malaya and the deserts of Arabia through the Falklands to the streets of Belfast.

BRITAIN IS ONE OF ABOUT 90 nations to use a version of the Belgian FN FAL. Built under licence as the **L1A1 SLR** (self-loading rifle), it has been in service since the 1950s.

Unlike its Belgian counterpart, the SLR only fires semi-auto. The British Army, which puts a premium on marksmanship, feels that with full-power rounds accuracy is impossible when firing fully automatically.

Since the middle of the 1980s, the SLR has been replaced by the **SA80**. This is largely because the original rifles are getting old and have seen some

hard service, and many regiments have found teaching marksmanship with worn-out weapons to be an impossible task.

SPECIFICATION
Name: L1A1 SLR
Type: battle rifle
Calibre: 7.62-mm x 51 NATO
Weight: 4.3 kg
Dimensions: length 1143 mm; barrel length 533 mm
Muzzle velocity: 840 metres per second
Effective range: 600 m
Rate of fire: single-shot semi-auto only
Magazine: 20-round box
Users: Australia, Barbados, Canada, Gambia, Guyana, Malaysia, New Zealand, Oman, Singapore, UK

In service from the mid-1950s, the SLR was basically the FN FAL modified to suit British requirements.

SA80 Individual Weapon assault rifle

THE BRITISH ARMY WAS late to adopt a small-calibre battle rifle, in spite of the fact that much of the pioneering work on such weapons had been done in Britain. The 5.56-mm Enfield **SA80** Individual Weapon, designated **L85** by the British Army, entered service in the mid-1980s, replacing the L1A1 version of the classic FN FAL.

The SA80 is a 'bullpup' design. Mechanically, it is a conventional gas-operated gun, similar to the AR-18 Armalite. It is fed via M16-type magazines.

Short and handy, it shoots very well, and is well suited to urban combat and mechanised warfare. Equipped with a 4x optical sight, especially valuable when fighting in poor light, it is one of the most accurate assault rifles in service today.

Unfortunately its reliability is not of the same

A British soldier hangs his SA80 from its sling as he throws a grenade into an Iraqi bunker during the Gulf War. Its ease of handling should have made the SA80 a good battlefield weapon, but numerous faults, including a tendency for the magazines to fall out unexpectedly, meant that it did not have a successful combat debut.

high standard, and it is prone to break when used in combat conditions. This may explain the gun's lack of export success.

SPECIFICATION

Name: L85A1
Type: assault rifle
Calibre: 5.56-mm x 45 NATO
Weight: empty 3.8 kg
Dimensions: length 785 mm; barrel length 518 mm
Muzzle velocity: 940 metres per second
Effective range: 600 m
Rate of fire: 610-775 rpm (cyclic)
Magazine: 30-round box
Users: United Kingdom

Compact and very accurate, the SA80's only problem is its lack of reliability.

The SA80 is a bullpup design, with the magazine located behind the trigger.

USA
M1 Carbine light battle rifle

Manufactured by at least 10 companies during World War II, more M1 Carbines were built than any other single American military firearm.

SUPPLIED TO A US ORDNANCE Department requirement for a light rifle not exceeding five and a half pounds (2.5 kg) and capable of either self-loading or fully automatic fire, the light and handy **M1 Carbine** produced by Winchester in 1941 became standard issue to the US airborne forces during World War II. It was used extensively in the Pacific campaigns, and became very popular throughout the free world after the war ended.

The M1 Carbine incorporated a new form of gas operation, now known as short-stroke piston operation, developed in 1941 by Winchester for an experimental self-loading rifle. It used an intermediate-power cartridge adapted from a .32-calibre round dating from the beginning of the century. Known as the .30 SR M1 (SR standing for 'short rifle'), it later became identified with the only major weapon designed to fire it and is now known as the .30 M1 Carbine round.

Although the cartridge it fires is little more than a pistol round, the M1 Carbine is accurate at combat ranges and is easily controllable. Popular as an officer's sidearm as well, it was widely used in Asia after World War II – by French, then Vietnamese and US forces in Indo-China and by the British in Malaya.

Most M1s were semi-automatic, some with a folding stock being known as **M1A1**s, but over 500,000 fully automatic **M2** carbines were produced in 1944-45. There was also the night-fighting **M3**: fitted with a flash hider and designed to carry an infra-red night sight, only 2,100 were made. Total production is estimated to be 6,232,100.

SPECIFICATION
Name: M1 Carbine
Type: light battle rifle
Calibre: .30 Carbine (7.62-mm x 33)
Weight: empty 2.36 kg
Dimensions: length 904 mm; barrel length 458 mm
Muzzle velocity: 600 metres per second
Effective range: 300 m
Rate of fire: semi-auto (M1) or 750 rpm (M2)
Magazine: 15- or 30- round box
Users: obsolete, but still in second-line service all over South America and Asia

USA
M1 Garand battle rifle

The M1 gave American GIs in World War II an advantage over other soldiers armed with manually-operated bolt-action weapons.

service or reserve in several countries from Central America to Southeast Asia.

SPECIFICATION
Name: M1
Type: battle rifle
Calibre: .30-06 (7.62-mm x 63)
Weight: empty 4.3 kg
Dimensions: length 1106 mm; barrel length 610 mm
Muzzle velocity: 865 metres per second
Effective range: 600 m
Rate of fire: semi-automatic
Magazine: 8-round clip
Users: may still be found active or reserve in a dozen countries, including Chile, Costa Rica, Denmark, Greece, Guatemala, Haiti, Honduras, Italy, the Philippines Taiwan, Tunisia, Turkey and with the US National Guard

THE FIRST SELF-LOADING RIFLE to become the standard service weapon in any army, the **M1 Garand** was adopted by the US Army in 1932 and issued in quantity four years later. Used by the US Army throughout World War II and Korea, some 5.5 million M1s had been made by the 1950s.

Still a popular target-shooting rifle in the USA and now produced by Springfield Armory, the M1 was supplied to many US allies, including South Vietnam and Italy, where it was made under licence by Beretta. More than four million were turned out by US arsenals during World War II, with a further 500,000 completed during the Korean War.

A big, strong rifle, the M1 earned its reputation for reliability under combat conditions from the jungles of the Philippines to the frozen hills of Korea. Although obsolescent, Garands can still be found in

Designed in the late 1920s, the M1 was the first self-loading rifle to go into large-scale military service.

M14 battle rifle

IN THE 1950s THE AMERICANS persuaded all NATO armies to adopt their .30-calibre cartridge as the 7.62-mm x 51 mm NATO standard. They needed a new rifle to fire it, however, so in 1957 US troops began to receive the **M14** battle rifle.

Although manufactured to very high standards and capable of great accuracy, the M14 was a throwback to World War II. It was basically an M1 Garand chambered to fire the new round, with a removable 20-round box magazine in place of the M1's clip-loaded fixture, and the addition of a selective-fire capability.

However, in service it was discovered that prolonged automatic fire overheated the barrel and that accuracy could not be maintained. Most M14s were altered to provide semi-automatic fire only. The fully automatic **M14A1** was designed as a squad support weapon and had a bipod and pistol grip, but barrel heating was still a problem.

Used by the Marine Corps in the early days of

The M14's major combat usage was in Vietnam. In addition to the standard rifle, the much less-common M14A1 fully automatic version seen here saw action with the US Army and Marines.

the Vietnam War, the M14 was rapidly replaced by the 5.56-mm M16, in spite of the protests of old-school soldiers who decried the new fast-shooting, smaller-calibre weapons.

The M14 remains in second-line service, but apart from specialist variants used by snipers, who make good use of its long range and accuracy, the M14 had one of the shortest front-line careers of any modern rifle.

SPECIFICATION

Name: M14
Type: battle rifle
Calibre: 7.62-mm x 51 NATO
Weight: empty 3.88 kg
Dimensions: length 1120 mm; barrel length 559 mm
Muzzle velocity: 853 metres per second
Effective range: 600 m
Rate of fire: M14 single-shot semi-auto; selective-fire versions 700-750 rpm (cyclic)
Magazine: 20-round box
Users: South Korea, Taiwan, USA

The M14 was a solid, accurate rifle which was really too powerful to be a fully effective battlefield assault weapon.

Marines in Vietnam kept the M14 longer than the US Army, until replaced by the lightweight M16.

AR-15/M-16 assault rifle

THE **AR-15** WAS ONE OF THE FIRST of the modern 5.56-mm calibre rifles to enter service. Designed by Eugene Stoner for the Armalite company in the late 1950s, the AR-15 made extensive use of pressed steel and plastic in its construction.

Although it looked like a toy, the AR-15 was a serious weapon. Firing high-velocity 5.56-mm ammunition, much smaller than the then standard 7.62-mm NATO round, it allowed soldiers to carry more ammunition into combat. The rifle was designated **M16** when issued to the US Air Force in the mid-1960s, and as the **M16A1** was to go on to achieve fame as the US Army's standard rifle in

The M16 was one of the many new weapons introduced during the Vietnam War. It made a great impact, being instantly recognisable on screen in the first 'television war'.

Vietnam. However, the British were among the first to use the weapon in combat, in Borneo.

After initial reliability problems the M16 proved to be an effective battlefield weapon, and the current **M16A2** variant is much improved.

Although prone to damage, M16 magazines have become standard fittings, and most modern assault rifles will accept them.

SPECIFICATION
Name: M16A1
Type: assault rifle
Calibre: 5.56-mm x 45 NATO
Weight: empty 3.18 kg
Dimensions: length 990 mm; barrel length 508 mm
Muzzle velocity: 1000 metres per second
Effective range: 400 m
Rate of fire: 700-950 rpm (cyclic)
Magazine: 20- or 30- round box
Users: 55 countries worldwide including Chile, Dominican Republic, Haiti, Italy, Jordan, South Korea, Mexico, Nicaragua, Panama, the Philippines, UK, USA and Vietnam

The M16's straight-through design with high-set sights made for instinctively accurate aiming.

USA
M16A2 assault rifle

As with other models of the M16, the M16A2 is available in various sizes. The M4 Carbine is a lighter and shorter variant with reduced barrel and a sliding stock. The Colt Commando seen here is even smaller, about the size of a sub-machine gun.

US Army versions fire three-round bursts, but not fully automatically. Still as light and handy as the original, but more accurate and longer-ranged, the M16A2 is a first-class, modern assault rifle.

EUGENE STONER'S REVOLUTIONARY **AR-15** design first entered widespread service in the 1960s. After initial teething troubles, it became the standard by which other small-calibre, high-velocity assault rifles were judged. After 20 years, however, it was starting to show its age.

The **M16A2** is essentially the M16 modified to fire the harder-hitting SS109 round that has become standard in NATO. The weapon retains the earlier version's light weight and ease of handling, but incorporates a number of improvements. It is more solidly built, adding durability, and a heavier barrel promotes greater accuracy than preceding M16s.

SPECIFICATION
Name: M16A2
Type: assault rifle
Calibre: 5.56-mm x 45 NATO
Weight: empty 3.4 kg
Dimensions: length 1000 mm; barrel length 510 mm
Muzzle velocity: 950 metres per second
Effective range: 600 m
Rate of fire: 700-900 rpm (cyclic)
Magazine: 20- or 30-round box
Users: US armed forces and replacing M16A1 worldwide

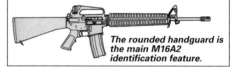

The rounded handguard is the main M16A2 identification feature.

USA
Mini-14 assault rifle

Although its wooden furniture gives the Mini-14 an old-fashioned look, it is nevertheless a modern and very effective assault rifle.

STURM, RUGER & COMPANY have been producing high-quality handguns and hunting rifles for many years. The **Ruger Mini-14** was one of their first forays into the military market, and differs considerably from the pressed-steel, sheet metal and plastic weapons typical of modern design.

Introduced in the early 1970s, the Mini-14 resembles a scaled-down version of the M14 battle rifle, although a number of changes have been made to allow the weapon to cope with the higher chamber pressures generated in firing high-velocity 5.56-mm rounds. High-quality wood furniture and a blued steel finish ensure that the rifle looks like a product from a previous age, although in most respects it is a thoroughly modern weapon which has been carefully engineered to prevent dust and debris entering the action.

Although a commercial design originally intended for hunting, the Mini-14 has found numerous police and security applications. The **Mini-14/20GB** is a militarised variant, incorporating a bayonet lug, flash suppressor and a heat-resistant ventilated glass-reinforced plastic handguard. Like the original rifle, it is available in both blued and stainless steel versions.

More overtly military, the **AC-556** looks like a Mini-14/20GB, but is a selective-fire weapon capable of semi-auto, three-round burst and full-auto fire. A more unusual variant is the **Mini-Thirty**, chambered for the standard Soviet 7.62 x 39-mm round, as fired by the famous Kalashnikov.

Light and handy, the Mini-14 is an extremely well-made piece which has found favour with police and security forces around the world.

SPECIFICATION
Name: Mini-14
Type: assault and security rifle
Calibre: 5.56-mm x 45 NATO
Weight: empty 2.9 kg
Dimensions: length 946 mm; barrel length 470 mm
Muzzle velocity: 1005 metres per second
Effective range: 300 m
Rate of fire: Mini-14, semi-auto only; AC-556, 750 rpm (cyclic)
Magazine: 5-, 20- or 30-round box
Users: many police and security forces around the world

AR-18 assault rifle

THE **AR-18** WAS DEVELOPED in the early 1960s by the Armalite company. It is not a variant of the AR-15, although it uses some of the ideas from the earlier AR-15/M16 series.

Designed as a cheap, alternative weapon for countries that could not afford the latest Western technology, it utilises steel stampings where the earlier Armalite designs employed expensive aluminium forgings. The AR-18 is easier to maintain, easier to clean and more reliable than the M16.

Unfortunately, it could not compete with the ubiquitous M16A1 and the AK-47, which were available all over the world in huge numbers. Licence manufacture was carried out in Singapore, which went on to produce its own weapons

The AR-18 is a cheap but highly effective assault rifle. It did not sell as well as it might have done, but its ease of use made it popular with both security forces and terrorist organisations.

designs, and the UK, but without any great commercial success.

The AR-18 is nevertheless a light, accurate, easy-to-handle assault rifle. The rotary bolt and gas piston have been copied to some extent in the British SA80 bullpup assault rifle.

Although similar to the AR-15, the AR-18 has a more basic appearance. One difference is that to take up less space its butt can be folded along the right-hand side of the receiver.

SPECIFICATION

Name: AR-18
Type: assault rifle
Calibre: 5.56-mm x 45 NATO
Weight: empty 3.17 kg
Dimensions: length 940 mm; barrel length 464 mm
Muzzle velocity: 1000 metres per second
Effective range: 450 m
Rate of fire: 800 rpm (cyclic)
Magazine: 20-, 30- or 40-round box
Users: some commercial sales; used by several police forces and a small number of military organisations

The AR-18 retains the 'inline' design of barrel, receiver and butt seen on earlier Armalite rifle designs.

AK-47 assault rifle

BATTLE ANALYSIS OF INFANTRY combat in World War II showed that most fighting took place at close range. As a result, in the late 1940s the Soviets fielded the **Avtomat Kalashnikova (AK-47)**. Firing a lower-powered cartridge than the rifles it replaced, the AK was designed for battlefield ranges of under 300 metres, which had been shown to cover 90 per cent of all combat.

Built simply but solidly, the AK-47's capacity for automatic fire and exceptional reliability made it a superior infantry weapon.

Easy to maintain and easy to use, rifles of the AK family have proved ideal for arming conscripts and poorly trained soldiers in Third World armies.

More Avtomat Kalashnikova or AK assault rifles have been built and have seen combat than any other firearm in history.

In 1959 the USSR adopted an improved version, designated **Modernizirovannyi Avtomat Kalashnikova** or **AKM**. Contrary to normal Soviet practice, the AK-47 used fairly expensive machined components. Cheaper and easier to produce, the AKM was largely of stamped steel construction.

Although supplanted from the late 1970s by the smaller-calibre AK-74, many reserve units in former Soviet and Warsaw Pact states are still equipped with the AKM. The AK series is the most widely manufactured military rifle of all time, with as many as 30 million guns having been built.

The Kalashnikov's 'banana' magazine has become its most characteristic recognition feature.

SPECIFICATION

Name: AK-47
Type: assault rifle
Calibre: 7.62-mm x 39 Soviet
Weight: empty 4.3 kg
Dimensions: length 869 mm; barrel length 414 mm
Muzzle velocity: 710 metres per second
Effective range: 300 m
Rate of fire: 600 rpm (cyclic)
Magazine: 30-round box
Users: most widely used weapon in the world, found in over 100 countries in military and guerrilla hands

AK-74 assault rifle

AS WESTERN ARMIES ADOPTED weapons in 5.56-mm calibre, the Soviets re-equipped with the **AK-74**, a new version of the AKM.

It is operated like all other Kalashnikov rifles, but fires a 5.45-mm cartridge which produces almost no recoil. It feels much the same as firing a .22 target rifle but the 5.45-mm bullet travels at high velocity, and is designed to deform when it strikes the target. Its wounding capacity is similar to that of a soft-nosed bullet.

The AK-74 looks very similar to the AKM but has

The AK-74 was introduced in the 1970s. It was basically the preceding AKM with minimum changes made to enable it to fire the then new smaller-calibre high-velocity 5.45-mm round.

a groove running along the stock and foregrip. Its most notable identification features are the standard orange or brown plastic magazines and the prominent muzzle brake. This deflects the rifle's fearsome muzzle blast to the sides, which is bad news for the ears of someone standing next to the firer.

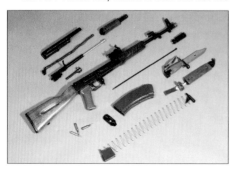

A field-stripped AK-74 demonstrates the small number of working parts which make the Kalashnikov series so easy to maintain.

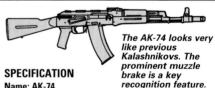

The AK-74 looks very like previous Kalashnikovs. The prominent muzzle brake is a key recognition feature.

SPECIFICATION

Name: AK-74
Type: assault rifle
Calibre: 5.45-mm x 39 Soviet
Weight: empty 3.6 kg
Dimensions: length 930 mm; barrel length 400 mm
Muzzle velocity: 900 metres per second
Effective range: 400 m
Rate of fire: 650 rpm (cyclic)
Magazine: 30-round box
Users: former Soviet republics, some ex-Warsaw Pact forces

AKSU assault rifle

On full auto, the AKSU is a good 'bullet hose', pumping out a lot of high-velocity rounds in a short time. But with such a short barrel, it is very hard to control.

FIRST SEEN IN THE WEST in the early 1980s, when some were captured in Afghanistan, the **AKSU** is a shortened version of the Kalashnikov AK-74 assault rifle. Like the Colt Commando version of the M16, it retains the same grips, breech mechanism and magazine as the full-size rifle, but has a drastically shortened barrel.

Another weapon which treads the no-man's land between assault rifles and sub-machine guns, the AKSU was issued to vehicle and helicopter crews as well as to the Soviet airborne and Spetsnaz forces that played such a leading role in counter-insurgency operations in Afghanistan.

Unlike previous AK designs, the receiver cover is permanently attached, hinging at the front. Otherwise the working parts are the same as on the full length AK-74 rifle. Within 200 metres or so its

performance as a semi-automatic weapon is quite adequate. The combined muzzle brake and flash hider is essential to moderate what would otherwise be an awesome muzzle blast; even so, firing high-velocity rounds through such a short barrel means that fully automatic fire is alarmingly unselective.

Easily concealed, thanks to its folding stock and compact dimensions, the AKSU will no doubt play its part in the realignment of post-communist Asia.

SPECIFICATION
Name: AKSU
Type: assault rifle
Calibre: 5.45-mm x 39 Soviet
Weight: empty 3.1 kg
Dimensions: length 675 mm, butt extended; barrel length 200 mm
Muzzle velocity: 800 metres per second
Effective range: 200 m
Rate of fire: 800 rpm (cyclic)
Magazine: 30-round box
Users: former Soviet republics

SKS assault rifle

North Vietnamese soldiers armed with Chinese-made copies of the SKS take part in the final assault on Saigon in 1975.

retaining them for ceremonial duties only.

China still manufactures a copy of the SKS known as the Type 56 Carbine. Originally a purely military weapon equipped with a spike bayonet, it is now for sale as a sporting rifle.

SPECIFICATION
Name: SKS
Type: assault rifle
Calibre: 7.62-mm x 39 Soviet
Weight: empty 3.8 kg
Dimensions: length 1021 mm; barrel length 520 mm
Muzzle velocity: 735 metres per second
Effective range: 400 m
Rate of fire: single-shot semi-auto
Magazine: 10-round box
Users: former Soviet republics, China, several countries in Asia

THE **SAMORAZYADNYI KARABIN SIMONOVA** or SKS was the first weapon designed to fire the German-inspired Soviet 7.62-mm intermediate-power assault rifle round. Solidly made, simple to operate and immensely strong, the SKS was manufactured in large numbers all over the Communist world.

Capable of reasonable accuracy to about 400 metres, the SKS was supplied to most Soviet-equipped armies, and has been widely used in Africa, the Middle East and Southeast Asia. But because the AK-47 proved so successful, the Soviets abandoned the SKS within a few years,

The SKS was a good enough design which had the misfortune to appear just before the revolutionary AK-47.

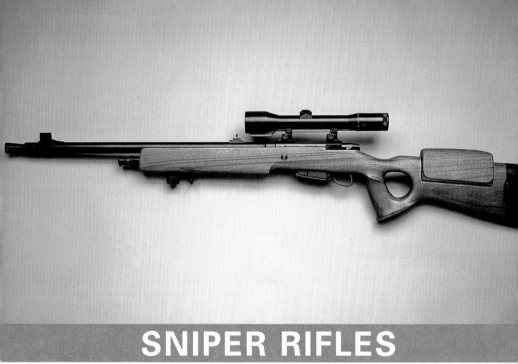

SNIPER RIFLES

AUSTRIA
SSG 69 sniper rifle

MANUFACTURED IN AUSTRIA by Steyr-Daimler-Puch, the **Scharfschutzengewehr 69** or **SSG 69** is one of a long line of rifles from Steyr. Introduced into service in 1969, hence the designation, the SSG 69 is the standard sniping rifle of the Austrian army and is also employed by several foreign military and police units.

The SSG 69 differs from most modern bolt-action weapons of this type in that it uses the traditional Austrian Mannlicher rear-locking bolt rather than the Mauser-type forward-locking bolt. Developed from a sporting and target rifle, the SSG is an excellent and accurate weapon.

The barrel is cold-forged – a method pioneered by Steyr in which the rifling is hammered into the bore using a mandrel. The five-round rotary magazine employed on Mannlicher's World War I-era rifles has been retained, although a 10-round box was also made. The latter is no longer in production due to changes in UIT competition shooting that reduced the demand from civilian sports shooters.

The SSG is a solid, traditional design capable of great accuracy, which is available in both police and military versions.

The stock is made of synthetic material and is adjustable in length to suit the firer. The double-pressure trigger is also adjustable.

The standard military version of the SSG can produce 40-cm groups at 800 metres; the heavy-barrel match model can do even better. Delivered from the factory with a Kahles ZF69 telescopic sight offering x6 magnification and calibrated to 800 metres, the SSG can also accept a wide range of optical, electronic and night-sighting devices. Simple iron sights are brazed onto the barrel for emergency use.

SPECIFICATION
Name: Scharfschutzengewehr 69
Type: sniper rifle
Calibre: 7.62-mm x 51 NATO or .243 Winchester
Weight: 4.6 kg with telescope
Dimensions: length 1140 mm; barrel length 650 mm
Muzzle velocity: 860 metres per second
Sights: x6 telescope adjustable to 800 m
Effective range: 800 m
Magazine: 5-round rotary box
Users: Austrian army and several other armies and police forces in Europe and around the world

FRANCE
FR-F2 sniper rifle

Originally chambered for 7.5-mm ammunition, the current version of the French army's sniping rifle uses NATO standard 7.62-mm rounds.

barrel interfering with the shooter's sight picture.

Designed to achieve a first-round hit on a man-sized target at 600 metres, in capable hands the FR-F2 can group all 10 shots within 20 cm. At 200 metres, it groups to within 5 cm.

THE **FR-F2** IS THE CURRENT French sniper rifle. It is a development of the **FR-F1**, first issued in 1966 and chambered for the pre-war 7.5-mm x 54 cartridge used only in France. Although some were modified to fire 7.62-mm NATO, the rifle was only used by French forces.

The FR-F2 introduced some significant changes. Apart from the inevitable switch to NATO standard 7.62-mm ammunition, it has the bipod just forward of the magazine so the sniper can adjust it without having to move out of the firing position. The fore-end is made of metal, not wood, and is covered in matt-black plastic. The barrel is sheathed in a plastic thermal sleeve, which minimises the weapon's infra-red signature and prevents the heat from the

SPECIFICATION
Name: Fusil à répétition Modèle F1
Type: sniper rifle
Calibre: 7.62-mm x 51 NATO or 7.5-mm x 54 Cartouche 1929 or Modèle 36
Weight: 5.2 kg
Dimensions: length 1138 mm; barrel length 552 mm
Muzzle velocity: 850 metres per second
Sights: x4 telescope
Effective range: 800 m
Magazine: 10-round box
Users: France

The FR-F2's bipod is mounted further back than on most sniping rifles.

Heckler & Koch sniper rifles

Most of the military sniping rifles offered by Heckler & Koch use the company's patented roller locking system.

reticle with six sight settings, from 100 to 600 metres. It fires standard 7.62-mm x 51 NATO ammunition, match grade for maximum accuracy.

HECKLER & KOCH HAS BEEN ringing the changes on its basic 7.62-mm G3 rifle design for 30 years, stretching and contracting its roller-locking system to cover a range from pistols through sub-machine guns and sniper rifles to general-purpose machine-guns. Sniper variants of the G3 include the **G3 AZF** and the **G3 SG/1**. More heavily modified versions of the G3 include the **MSG90**, and the very accurate **PSG 1**.

The PSG 1 has a heavy barrel, adjustable butt and trigger. It is semi-automatic only, with a five- or 20-round magazine, and the otherwise noisy action of the working parts has been specially silenced. The x6 zoom telescopic sight has an illuminated

SPECIFICATION
Name: Präzisionsschützengewehr 1
Type: sniper rifle
Calibre: 7.62-mm x 51 NATO (.308 Winchester Match)
Weight: 9 kg with sight
Dimensions: length 1208 mm; barrel length 650 mm with muzzle brake
Muzzle velocity: 820 metres per second
Sights: x1.5-x6 zoom telescope
Effective range: 700 m
Magazine: 5- or 20-round box
Users: German Special Forces and police, and numerous other police forces

Heckler & Koch claims a shot dispersal of less than 80 mm at 300 m for the PSG 1.

WA 2000 sniper rifle

Looking more like a prop from 'Star Wars' than a rifle, the remarkable WA 2000 is nevertheless a highly accurate security weapon.

results out of weapon and sight, accurate ammunition must also be used. Walther decided that of all commercially available rounds the .300 Winchester Magnum offered the best combination of accuracy and performance at long ranges. Other calibres, such as 7.62-mm NATO and 7.5-mm Swiss, can be used with a change of bolt and barrel.

INTRODUCED IN 1981 by the long-established Walther company, the **WA 2000** made an immediate impact with its futuristic design, which would not have looked out of place in a science fiction movie. Sold as the 'Rolls-Royce' of sniper rifles, it comes with an appropriate price tag.

The WA 2000 is a gas-operated bullpup weapon. One of the most important parts of any rifle design is the barrel, and it is doubly important for precision shooting weapons. Walther chose to clamp the barrel rigidly to the frame front and rear, so that torque imparted by a bullet spinning through the bore would not lift the muzzle away from its intended point of aim. The barrel is fluted externally, making it resistant to vibration, and it lies in a straight line with the shoulder, which also helps to counter muzzle lift.

The normal telescopic sight used on the WA 2000 is the excellent Schmidt & Bender x2.5-x10 zoom, but other sights can easily be mounted. To get best

Although solidly made, the WA 2000 is hardly a combat rifle. It is heavy and much too expensive for general issue, and needs fine tuning and careful handling for maximum performance. But for police, internal security and counter-terrorism sniping it is highly effective.

SPECIFICATION
Name: WA 2000
Type: sniper rifle
Calibre: .300 (7.62-mm) Winchester Magnum
Weight: 8.31 kg with sight
Dimensions: length 905 mm; barrel length 650 mm
Muzzle velocity: 900 metres per second
Sights: x2.5-x10 zoom telescope
Effective range: 900 m
Magazine: 6-round box
Users: various unspecified police and special forces

ISRAEL
Galil Sniper sniper rifle

The Galil Sniper is a highly accurate development of the Galil assault rifle. As a result, it is very tough and battleworthy.

THE **GALIL SNIPER RIFLE** RESEMBLES the assault rifle from which it was developed, and shares the ruggedness and relative simplicity of design handed down from the Kalashnikov which was its inspiration.

But the sniper version of the Galil has been redesigned and manufactured to the finest tolerances. The Galil sniper rifle is fitted with a heavy barrel to which has been added a muzzle brake/compensator. The solid butt, which can be folded forwards for carriage, has an adjustable butt pad and cheek rest, while a Nimrod x6 sight is standard. The sight can be replaced by a night sight without disturbing the weapon's zeroing.

The Galil's assault rifle descent suits it to the

rigours of combat better than many more modern, super-accurate but fragile rifles. Using the attached bipod, the Galil can group rounds in a 30-cm circle at 600 metres, which is more than adequate for most sniping purposes.

The Galil uses a modified Kalashnikov action, and is notable for its reliability.

SPECIFICATION
Name: Galil
Type: sniper rifle
Calibre: .7.62-mm x 51 NATO Match grade
Weight: 6.4 kg including bipod and sling
Dimensions: length 1115 mm; barrel length 508 mm without muzzle brake
Muzzle velocity: 815 metres per second
Sights: x6 telescope
Effective range: 700 m
Magazine: 20-round box
Users: Israel Defence Forces

ITALY
Beretta Sniper sniper rifle

Built to a very high standard, the Beretta Sniper is an orthodox weapon which incorporates some advanced features to enhance accuracy.

WHEN THE MARKET FOR HIGH-PRECISION sniper rifles expanded in the 1970s, most major European small-arms manufacturers produced designs. The Italian firm of Beretta was no exception, although its weapon appeared later than some of the competition and has never received a numerical designation.

Compared to many of the 'space age' designs, the **Beretta Sniper** is an orthodox, manually operated bolt-action rifle, which is built to the usual high Beretta standard. In common with other precision weapons it has a thumb-hole pattern stock, and the butt and cheek rest are adjustable to suit the firer. The hand stop on the underside of the forestock is also adjustable.

In spite of its conventional appearance, the Beretta Sniper has a number of advanced features. The heavy, free-floating barrel is designed to dampen any unwanted vibration, and a bipod can be fitted for stability. The tube under the barrel onto which the bipod fits also contains a device called a harmonic balancer, a forward-pointing counter-

weight which acts as a damper against vibrations of the barrel on firing and which offers superbly consistent shooting.

The Beretta Sniper has a NATO standard sight mount, and can take any NATO telescopic, low-light or infra-red sight. Standard equipment recommended by the manufacturer is the Zeiss Diavari x1.5-x6 zoom scope. Unlike other specialist sniper rifles, the Beretta Sniper is also equipped with fully adjustable precision match sights, so that even if the main sight is unserviceable a good shot should be able to hit a man-sized target at ranges of 300 metres or more.

SPECIFICATION
Name: Beretta Sniper
Type: sniper rifle
Calibre: 7.62-mm x 51 NATO Match
Weight: 7.2 kg with sight and bipod
Dimensions: length 1165 mm; barrel length 586 mm
Muzzle velocity: 860 metres per second
Sights: x1.5-x6 zoom telescope
Effective range: 800 m
Magazine: 5-round box
Users: various unspecified police and special forces

L42A1 sniper rifle

The rugged and reliable L42 is a modified World War II vintage rifle. Although obsolescent, it is still capable of delivering accurate long-range fire.

THE BRITISH ARMY INVESTED little time in sniper training during the 1960s, but the Royal Marines maintained an excellent sniper training programme that came to influence the Army when it 'rediscovered' sniping. Until the late 1980s, British snipers used the **L42A1** – a version of the famous Lee-Enfield bolt-action weapon carried by British infantry since 1895.

The Lee-Enfield was one of the toughest and most reliable battle rifles of the century, and could be fired with great accuracy. During World War II the standard telescopic sniping variant was the **No. 4 Mk 1(T)**, which was chambered for the long-serving British .303 cartridge.

After the war, these rifles were converted to fire the new NATO standard 7.62-mm ammunition and given the new designation. The modification entailed fitting new barrels, new magazines, some changes to the trigger mechanisms and cutting down the forestocks. Open sights were retained as well, and eight different sized foresights were

provided for zeroing. Although the stock terminated about halfway along the barrel, both were invariably shrouded in hessian and/or scrim scarf to camouflage the tell-tale shape of the rifle.

Used in action with distinction from the Middle East to the Falklands, the L42A1 has now been outclassed by the latest high-tech rifles available from a number of manufacturers. But it is still a sturdy, reliable and reasonably accurate weapon capable of giving good service. Fitted with a commercial zoom sight, it is used as a police weapon and is known as the **Enfield Enforcer**.

SPECIFICATION
Name: L42A1
Type: sniper rifle
Calibre: 7.62-mm x 51 NATO
Weight: 4.43 kg
Dimensions: length 1181 mm; barrel length 699 mm
Muzzle velocity: 838 metres per second
Sights: x4 telescope
Effective range: 800 m
Magazine: 10-round box
Users: British forces and police

M.85 sniper rifle

Parker Hale rifles are built to a very high standard, and serve with several Commonwealth armies.

5,000 rounds. The trigger is adjustable for weight and pull, and the butt can be altered to suit the firer. A suppressor can be fitted for clandestine use.

The Model 85 can take a variety of telescopes and vision devices, but with a standard x6 sight it should guarantee first-round hits at 600 metres and 85 per cent hit probability at ranges up to 900 metres.

THE BRITISH FIRM OF PARKER HALE has been in the business of manufacturing competition and hunting rifles for many years. It was a natural step to go on to produce sniper rifles for military and security use.

The **Model 82** with its Mauser-style bolt-action was for several years their most successful product, and became the standard sniper rifle in several Commonwealth countries. The design was bought by Navy Arms in the United States, and it was replaced in production by the **M.85**.

The M.85 has a Mauser-style bolt action allied to a heavy free-floating barrel guaranteed accurate for

SPECIFICATION
Name: M.85
Type: sniper rifle
Calibre: 7.62-mm x 51 NATO Match
Weight: 5.7 kg with sight
Dimensions: length 1150 mm; barrel length 700 mm
Muzzle velocity: 850 metres per second
Sights: x6 telescope
Effective range: 900 m
Magazine: 10-round box
Users: Australia, Canada, New Zealand

Militarised Parker-Hales generally have GRP or composite stocks.

L96A1 PM sniper rifle

Above: The PM is very different from the Lee-Enfield it has replaced in British Army service. It is a thoroughly modern high-tech design, incorporating aluminium and composite parts.

Left: The PM has been designed for use in the field, its manufacturers claiming that it will remain accurate even when its barrel has been fouled.

DESIGNED AND MANUFACTURED by the firm of Accuracy International, the high-technology **PM sniper rifle system** has replaced the long-serving Lee-Enfield L42 rifle in British service. Designated **L96A1** by the British Ministry of Defence, the PM is issued to Army and Royal Marine snipers.

The bolt-action weapon fulfils the British forces' requirement for a guaranteed hit at 600 yards. It is designed to put its first round on target in any conditions, even when fouled by heavy use. The

stainless steel barrel of the L96A1 is free-floating within the ambidextrous stock. The rifle has an integral bipod and it can also be fitted with a retractable spike under the butt. The trigger too can be removed and adjusted without dismantling the entire weapon.

The standard Schmidt & Bender sight offers x6 magnification, but it can be replaced for counter-terrorist work by a x10 fixed sight and a x2.5-x10 zoom sight. Infantry versions of the rifle are also equipped with fully adjustable target quality iron sights, graduated out to 700 metres.

The makers offer other versions of the rifle, including the **'Covert PM'**, which has an integral full-length suppressor. This has an effective range of 300 metres using subsonic 7.62-mm ammunition. There is also a **Super Magnum** version which fires .338 Lapua Magnum, .300 Winchester Magnum or 7-mm Remington Magnum. All three calibres offer light armour penetration and an effective range significantly greater than the 7.62-mm version.

The most recent variant is the **Model AW** sniper rifle. A product-improved PM, the AW equips the Swedish army, where it is known as the **PSG90**. Among other improvements it has anti-freeze mechanisms, and four years of Arctic trials have ensured that the weapon functions under all conditions. It has also been designed to fire a new generation of saboted sniper ammunition, offering great accuracy and penetration. It will probably be acquired by the British Army when orders for the L96A1 have been filled.

The PM system fully meets the British Army's requirement for a first-round hit at 600 metres and accurate harassing fire at 1000 metres.

SPECIFICATION
Name: L96A1 PM
Type: sniper rifle
Calibre: 7.62-mm x 51 NATO Match
Weight: 6.5 kg with sight
Dimensions: length 1124 mm; barrel length 655 mm
Muzzle velocity: 850 metres per second
Sights: x6 telescope
Effective range: 1000 m
Magazine: 6-round box
Users: United Kingdom, Sweden, and an unspecified number of countries in Africa, Asia, and the Middle East

M21 sniper rifle

ALTHOUGH THE US ARMY was one of the first to adopt a small-calibre weapon as its standard infantry rifle, it retained a full-power weapon firing the 7.62-mm NATO cartridge for its snipers. The **M21 US Rifle** is the standard sniping rifle of the US Army. Though it will eventually be replaced by the new M24 Sniper Weapon system, it is likely to remain in service for years to come.

The M21 is an enhanced version of the Army's battle rifle of the 1950s and 1960s, the 7.62-mm M14. Originally known as the **Rifle, M14, National Match (Accurized)**, the M21 retains the appearance and basic mechanism of its progenitor but uses a heavy barrel. Only selected barrels manufactured to the closest tolerances are fitted to the M21.

The hand-assembled trigger mechanism is adjusted to provide a crisp and consistent release. The gas-operation mechanism has also been worked over for smoothness of action. The x3-x9

Although the M14 battle rifle from which it was developed was not a great success, the M21 is a much better weapon which has served the US Army well for many years.

zoom telescopic sight has the usual cross-hairs, but it also has a system of graticules that allows the sniper to judge accurately the distance to a man-sized target.

In competent hands the M21 is expected to put 10 rounds in a 15-cm group at 300 metres, and can hit a man-sized target at almost a kilometre.

SPECIFICATION

Name: M21 US rifle
Type: sniper rifle
Calibre: 7.62-mm x 51 NATO Match
Weight: 5.6 kg with sight
Dimensions: length 1120 mm; barrel length 560 mm
Muzzle velocity: 850 metres per second
Sights: x3-x10 zoom telescope
Effective range: 900 m
Magazine: 20-round box
Users: US armed forces, US police forces, various police and special forces in Latin America and Southeast Asia

The M21 uses a modified Garand action originally developed in the 1930s.

The M21 was originally fitted with a x3 telescope, but this has been replaced by a zoom sight.

Remington 700 sniper rifle

Above: Designed as a hunting rifle, the Remington 700 remains a popular weapon on the American civilian market.

Left: Some 2,500 examples of the new M24 weapon system are to be acquired. The new weapons will equip all US Army and Special Forces snipers.

commercial hunting weapon most nearly met their requirements.

The **Remington 700** has a Mauser-type bolt action, a five-round magazine, and is normally fitted with a x3-x9 zoom telescopic sight. Taken into service as the **M40**, the rifle gave satisfactory service, although even with the gloss taken off its wooden furniture and blued metal its civilian ancestry remained evident.

Combat experience pointed out the need for some modification to the basically civil design to make it more suitable for the hard use it was getting with the Marines, and the militarised version of the rifle was given the designation **M40A1**.

On the M40A1 the original barrel has been replaced by a heavier stainless steel tube. The wooden stock has been replaced by less aesthetic but cheaper and more practical glass-reinforced plastic, and a new x10 sight fitted as standard.

The current US Army military sniping rifle is also based on the long bolt-action of the Remington 700, although its adjustable Kevlar-graphite stock gives it a different appearance. First delivered in the late 1980s and gradually replacing the long-serving M21 rifle, the **M24 Sniper Weapon System** has been developed as a complete package. Rifle, bipod, day sight, night sight, iron sights, deployment kit, cleaning kit, carrying case and telescope case are carried in a complete system-carrying case. The M24 has a six-shot box magazine.

The M24 is destined to fulfil the needs of all the US services. Currently fitted with an M/40X custom trigger and chambered for selected 7.62 cartridges designated M118 Special Sniper Ball, it will also be available in .300 Winchester Magnum.

THE US MARINE CORPS employed variants of the M1 Garand for their snipers in the years after World War II, but when a replacement was required during the Vietnam War they found that a

Above: Service rifles descended from the Remington 700 are much more utilitarian in appearance, with dulled metal barrels and matt black or camouflaged plastic composite stocks.

SPECIFICATION

Name: M40A1
Type: sniper rifle
Calibre: 7.62-mm x 51 NATO
Weight: 6.57 kg
Dimensions: length 1117 mm; barrel length 610 mm
Muzzle velocity: 777 metres per second
Sights: x10 telescope
Effective range: 900 m
Magazine: 6-round box
Users: US Marine Corps (M40A1), US Army (M24 Sniper Weapon System)

Fifty-Calibre Sniper Rifles sniper rifle

MOST MODERN SNIPER RIFLES can make one-shot kills at between 600 and 900 metres. But for ultra-long-range sniping, you need something more. The something is the big 50-calibre round, designed for the M2 heavy machine-gun, which itself was used for sniping during the Vietnam War. Fifty-calibre weapons are guaranteed to cause massive injury and can do so at far greater range than is possible with conventional rifle ammunition. The penetration of the .50-calibre round also enables it to destroy light vehicles, aircraft and helicopters.

Since the mid-1980s, several manufacturers have supplied small quantities of .50-calibre rifles to the US Army, Navy, and Marine Corps. McMillan is best known in the USA for its tough, synthetic rifle stocks fitted to the US Marine Corps M40A1 sniper rifles. Since 1986, Marine rifles have also been fitted with the same trigger actions as McMillan's own 'Signature' sporting rifles. When the US Navy SEALs began to experiment with .50-calibre rifles, it requested McMillan to develop such a weapon. McMillan responded with the single-shot **M87 ELR**, which was soon followed by a five-round magazine version. Both are conventional rifles with thumb

The Barrett Model 90 is a bolt-action version of the Model 82. It is shorter and lighter than the semi-automatic versions, but retains the big rifle's excellent long-range performance.

Dwarfing the conventional Marine Corps sniping rifle alongside, the Macmillan M87 ELR has to be big to make the best use of the huge .50-calibre rounds it is designed to fire.

safety and an adjustable trigger. A massive muzzle brake diverts the blast of gas sideways.

The rival **Barrett Model 82A1** semi-automatic rifle proved more popular, however, and in September 1991 Barrett won an order for 300 of these huge rifles. The Model 82A1 overcomes the formidable recoil of the .50-calibre round by using a muzzle brake that diverts much of the propellant gas sideways. The Barrett .50-calibre sniper rifle was credited with a confirmed kill at 1800 metres during the Gulf War of 1991.

SPECIFICATIONS

Name: M87 ELR
Type: long-range sniper rifle
Calibre: .50-calibre Browning (12.7-mm x 99)
Weight: 9.5 kg
Dimensions: length 1346 mm; barrel length 736 mm
Muzzle velocity: 850 metres per second
Sights: x10 telescope
Effective range: 1500 metres
Magazine: 5-round box
Users: USA

Name: Barrett M82A1 'Light Fifty'
Type: sniper rifle
Calibre: .50 calibre Browning (12.7-mm x 99)
Weight: 12.9 kg
Dimensions: length 1448 mm; barrel length 737 mm
Muzzle velocity: 850 metres per second
Sights: x10 telescope
Effective range: 1800 m
Magazine: 10-round box
Users: USA, UK, others

SVD Dragunov sniper rifle

THE SOVIET ARMY ALWAYS recognised the value of the sniper for eliminating key enemy personnel at long range, and there is no reason to suppose that Russia and other ex-Soviet states think any differently. But since the Kalashnikov rifles and light machine-guns used by the rest of the platoon are not very accurate beyond 400 metres, a long-range weapon is essential.

For many years Soviet snipers used the Moisin-Nagant bolt-action rifle whose design dated back to the 1890s. But in the 1960s, a new weapon appeared in the shape of the **SVD** or **Dragunov** sniper rifle. The SVD uses the basic Kalashnikov action, simplified since full-auto fire is not required, and made smoother as is only sensible on a precision weapon. The action is modified to handle

The powerful and accurate SVD bears a strong resemblance to the Kalashnikov, and shares the AK's robust reliability.

In service with former Soviet republics and client states for more than three decades, the SVD or Dragunov is based on the famous Kalashnikov, suitably modified for higher-power cartridges.

the 7.62-mm x 54 rimmed cartridge used in Soviet machine-guns. Although the round dates back to the last century it is powerful, and modern versions are highly accurate. Equipped with a PSO-1 x4 scope, the Dragunov can achieve single-shot kills at 800 metres.

China produces a copy of the Dragunov, which is offered for export.

SPECIFICATION

Name: Snaiperskaya Vintovka Dragunova
Type: sniper rifle
Calibre: 7.62-mm x 54 rimmed
Weight: 4.3 kg
Dimensions: length 1225 mm; barrel length 622 mm
Muzzle velocity: 830 metres per second
Sights: x4 telescope
Effective range: 800 metres
Magazine: 10-round box
Users: former Soviet and ex-Warsaw Pact armies

Although similar to the Kalashnikov, the SVD's working parts can not be interchanged with other members of the family.

MACHINE-GUNS

MAG general-purpose machine-gun

WORLD WAR II ESTABLISHED the general-purpose machine-gun – a single weapon with the ability to be fired from a light bipod or even from a sling in the assault role, and from a heavy tripod in the defensive or sustained fire role, as a viable weapon. One of the best GPMGs ever produced is a product of the Belgian company of Fabrique National. Known as the **Mitrailleuse d'Appui Général**, or **MAG**, it is soundly engineered, very reliable, and has become the most widely used infantry weapon of its type in the world.

The MAG uses a conventional gas-operation system to fire NATO standard 7.62-mm cartridges. The tapping-off point beneath the barrel incorporates a gas regulator which allows the amount of

Possibly the finest machine-gun ever built, the FN MAG is in service with more than 75 countries around the world. Tough, accurate and reliable, it has been proved in combat from the Falklands to the Persian Gulf.

gas drawn off to be increased, ensuring that the weapon will function even when fouled by sustained use.

The MAG has been adapted to a variety of roles. With a butt and simple bipod it can be used as a somewhat heavy LMG. For sustained fire the butt is often removed and the gun is mounted on a heavy tripod. A quick-change barrel ensures that overheating is not a problem. It has been made with ribbed and smooth barrels, and with spade grips. It can also be used from a wide variety of mounts on vehicles, aircraft, helicopters and ships.

The FN MAG utilises a simple and effective belt-feed system inspired by the German MG42 of WWII.

SPECIFICATION

Name: Mitrailleuse d'Appui Général
Type: general-purpose machine-gun
Calibre: 7.62-mm x 51 NATO
Weight: 10.85 kg with butt and bipod; 22 kg with tripod
Dimensions: length 1255 mm; barrel length 545 mm
Muzzle velocity: 840 metres per second
Effective range: 1200 m
Rate of fire: 650-1000 rpm (cyclic)
Magazine capacity: belt fed
Users: more than 75 countries, including Belgium, Canada, Cuba, India, Israel, Libya, New Zealand, Peru, South Africa, Sweden, Uganda, UK, USA, Zimbabwe

Minimi squad support weapon

FABRIQUE NATIONAL OF BELGIUM produced one of the finest combat machine-guns ever in the shape of the FN MAG, so when they announced that they were developing a light machine-gun designed to fire the new NATO standard 5.56-mm round it was clearly a weapon to watch.

Using tried and tested mechanical systems, the gas-operated **Minimi** is fed by either disintegrating link belts, standard M16 magazines or 200-round belts, which are supplied in sturdy plastic boxes that clamp directly onto the gun. This helps to keep out mud and dirt.

For use from helicopters and other confined spaces, the smaller **Para Minimi** is available, with a sliding stock and shorter barrel. The Minimi was selected by the US Army as the **M249 Squad**

Designed by the company which produced the world-beating FN MAG, the Minimi is the squad support weapon of the US armed forces. It is much easier to use than the larger and heavier M60 GPMG it has replaced.

Automatic Weapon or **SAW**, and from 1984 it began replacing one M16 rifle in each infantry squad. With double the effective range of the M16, the M249 gives American infantrymen considerably greater firepower without the need for carrying heavy weapons or different-calibre ammunition.

The Minimi can be belt-fed, or it can accept M16-type assault rifle magazines without preparation.

SPECIFICATION

Name: Minimi
Type: squad support weapon
Calibre: 5.56-mm x 45 NATO
Weight: 6.85 kg
Dimensions: length 1040 mm; barrel length 465 mm
Muzzle velocity: 965 metres per second
Effective range: 600 m
Rate of fire: 700-1000 rpm (cyclic)
Magazine capacity: disintegrating link belt, 200-round belt, or 30-round M16-type box
Users: Australia, Belgium, Canada, Indonesia, Italy, USA, with several other nations currently testing the weapon with a view to purchase

The Minimi is smaller and lighter than the FN MAG, and is more suitable for assault use.

CZECH REPUBLIC

vz 59 general-purpose machine-gun

*ORIGINALLY PRODUCED AT BRNO in Czechoslovakia, the **vzor (model) 59** machine-gun continues in production now that the country has separated into the separate Czech and Slovak republics. The vz 59 continues the Czech tradition of manufacturing high-quality infantry weapons.*

Descended in part from the highly influential pre-war **ZB26** light machine-gun, which also evolved into the British Bren, the vz 59's immediate ancestor was the **vz 52**. This could be magazine- or belt-fed, and was classed as a light machine-gun. Analysis showed that the weapon was more often used as a belt-fed GPMG, and with the introduction of the vz 59 the magazine option was dropped.

The Czech army version of the vz 59 fires the Soviet 7.62-mm x 54R cartridge and uses a non-disintegrating link metal belt, which is more reliable than the ammunition belts used by its Soviet and Russian contemporaries.

The vz 59 is a general-purpose weapon in the high-quality tradition of Czech gun manufacture.

The model 59 has the usual GPMG options, a tripod mount and heavy barrel being available for sustained and anti-aircraft fire. It is also used as a coaxial machine-gun in tanks. With an eye to the export market, the Czechs produce the vz 59 chambered for 7.62-mm NATO. With the collapse of the Warsaw Pact it is likely that more NATO-calibre weapons will be produced by the Czech Republic's highly competent arms industry.

SPECIFICATION

Name: vz 59
Type: general-purpose machine-gun
Calibre: 7.62-mm x 54 rimmed Soviet or 7.62-mm x 51 NATO
Weight: 8.67 kg with bipod and light barrel; 19.24 kg with tripod and heavy barrel
Dimensions: length 1215 mm with heavy barrel; barrel length 693 mm
Muzzle velocity: 830 metres per second
Effective range: 1500 m (tripod) or 1000 m (bipod)
Rate of fire: 700-800 rpm, but barrel change required after 300-500 rounds
Magazine capacity: belt-fed
Users: Czech Republic, Slovakia

FRANCE

AA 52 NF-1 general-purpose machine-gun

An NF-1 gunner provides covering fire as French Foreign Legion paratroopers mount an attack.

THIS GENERAL-PURPOSE WEAPON was used by French troops during the Gulf War. An uninspired but reasonably effective weapon, it was designed primarily for cheap manufacture utilising metal stampings wherever possible.

Introduced in the wake of the French defeat in Indo-China, the original **AA 52** was chambered for the French 7.5-mm x 54 cartridge of 1929. Like the M60 the bipod was attached to the barrel, which is very inconvenient, and unlike the FN MAG it has to be carried cocked when a belt is in place.

The unique calibre meant that like many French weapons of the period the AA 52 could not fire the 7.62-mm ammunition now standard in the rest of

the world, and most guns still in service have been re-chambered and re-barrelled to the NATO calibre. The NF-1 model currently in production is built from new to fire 7.62-mm x 51 rounds.

SPECIFICATION

Name: Arme Automatique transformable modèle 52
Type: general-purpose machine-gun
Calibre: 7.5-mm x 54 or 7.62-mm x 51 NATO
Weight: 9.97 kg with bipod and light barrel; 21.97 kg with tripod and heavy barrel
Dimensions: length 1245 mm with heavy barrel and extended butt; barrel length 600 mm
Muzzle velocity: 830/840 metres per second
Effective range: 800 m (bipod); 1200 m (tripod)
Rate of fire: 700-900 rpm
Magazine capacity: belt-fed
Users: France and many former French colonies in Africa

The AA 52 can be supplied with heavy barrels for use in the sustained fire role.

GERMANY
MG3 general-purpose machine-gun

The MG 3 is a modernised version of the classic wartime MG 42, redesigned for ease of manufacture and rechambered to accept 7.62-mm NATO standard rounds.

GERMANY INTRODUCED THE FIRST true general-purpose machine-gun in the shape of the **MG34** before the start of World War II. It was replaced by the **MG42**, which used steel pressings in its manufacture where the earlier gun required expensive machined parts. The MG42 was a superb weapon with a very high rate of fire. This produced a distinctive sound, often described as being like ripping cloth, which was feared by opposing troops wherever they heard it.

The **MG 3** is the latest version of the the MG42. Manufactured by Rheinmetall, it is used by the German army and has been widely exported. It is also made under licence in Greece, Pakistan, Spain and Turkey. It retains the high rate of fire of the original gun, although the cyclic rate of fire can be varied depending upon whether the gun is fitted with light or a heavy bolt: the lighter the bolt, the faster

the weapon fires.

Although the basic design is now more than 50 years old, the MG 3 remains a highly efficient weapon. But the very high rate of fire imposes one major penalty, requiring frequent barrel changes. Even when firing short bursts, adding up to 250 rounds per minute, the user must change the barrel after 150 rounds – or once every 36 seconds.

The MG3 entered service with the West German army in 1968, succeeding earlier versions of the MG 42 which had been in service since the Federal Republic joined NATO in the 1950s.

SPECIFICATION
Name: Maschinengewehr 3
Type: general-purpose machine-gun
Calibre: 7.62-mm x 51 NATO
Weight: 11.05 kg with bipod
Dimensions: length 1225 mm; barrel length 565 mm
Muzzle velocity: 820 metres per second
Effective range: 2200 m (tripod) or 800 m (bipod)
Rate of fire: 700-1300 rpm
Magazine capacity: belt-fed
Users: Austria, Chile, Denmark, Greece, Iran, Italy, Norway, Pakistan, Portugal, Spain, Sudan, Turkey

Although the basic design is more than 50 years old, the MG 3 remains one of the finest GPMGs available in the 1990s.

GERMANY

HK21 general-purpose machine-gun

The HK21 is a derivative of Heckler & Koch's highly successful G3 assault rifle.

THE GERMAN FIRM OF HECKLER & KOCH manufactures a wide range of weapons based on the company's well-known roller locking system. The **HK21** is a belt-fed general-purpose machine-gun, which with the addition of an adaptor can use any of the magazines designed for H&K's G3 7.62-mm assault rifle. In fact the HK21 is closely-based on the rifle, and can fire single shots as well as fully automatic.

Although designed primarily as a squad automatic weapon, the HK21 can also be used as a GPMG. It has a quick and simple barrel-change facility which, when allied to a tripod mount, means that the gun can be used to provide sustained fire. A recoil booster allows the weapon to be used normally when firing blank cartridges, which is a useful training aid. Heckler & Koch also produces a variety of heavy-duty tripods as well as column and ring mounts to enable its guns to be used from vehicles.

The original version of the HK21 is no longer in production by the manufacturer, although the machine-gun is still built under licence in Portugal. In Germany it has been replaced by the **HK21A1**. This is a purely belt-fed weapon, the rarely used magazine adaptor having been abandoned. Heckler & Koch has developed a family of machine-guns using the same basic operating systems, including the magazine-fed **HK11A1**, the 5.56-mm calibre **HK23E**, and the current production **HK21E**. They are in service with many armies in Africa and Asia.

SPECIFICATION

Name: HK21E
Type: general-purpose machine-gun
Calibre: 7.62-mm x 51 NATO
Weight: 9.3 kg with bipod
Dimensions: length 1140 mm; barrel length 560 mm
Muzzle velocity: 840 metres per second
Effective range: 1200 m
Rate of fire: 800 rpm
Magazine capacity: belt-fed
Users: machine-guns based on the HK21 are used in Greece, Mexico, Portugal (where they are also built under licence) and in a number of African and Southeast Asian countries

---

SWITZERLAND

SIG 710 general-purpose machine-gun

The SIG 710-3 was one of the finest machine-guns ever built, but it was also one of the most costly, and was not adopted by the Swiss army.

SWISS GUN MANUFACTURE has always emphasised superb build quality over price and ease of manufacture. The **SIG 710** produced by the Schweizerische Industrie Gesellschaft (Swiss Industrial Corporation) is no exception

Originally a machine-gun variant of the Swiss army's model 57 assault rifle, the original **SIG 710-1**'s flash hider and perforated barrel jacket gave it the appearance of the German MG42, a version of which was in service with the Swiss army as the MG51. However, only the feed system was copied from the German weapon. The SIG design operates by delayed blowback, the delay mechanism utilising rollers rather like those used by Heckler & Koch.

The **SIG 710-2** had a carrying handle attached to the barrel, which was turned and pushed forwards to make a quick change. Development continued to the ultimate **SIG 710-3**, a superbly engineered general-purpose weapon, one of the most advanced in the world.

Manufactured to very high standards, the SIG 710 has the best barrel change of any GPMG, which can be completed even more quickly than on the German MG3 and is far easier to use in combat than that of the American M60.

Even though it makes use of modern manufacturing techniques, it is the very quality of the SIG 710 that worked against its export success. Such a high standard of manufacture comes at an equally high cost: like most Swiss personal weapons, the SIG 710 is very expensive and has won few export orders. It is no longer in production.

SPECIFICATION

Name: SIG 710-3
Type: general-purpose machine-gun
Calibre: 7.62-mm x 51 NATO
Weight: 11.29 kg with light barrel and bipod; 22.05 kg with heavy barrel and tripod
Dimensions: length 1143 mm; barrel length 559 mm
Muzzle velocity: 790 metres per second
Effective range: 800 m (bipod); 2200 m (tripod)
Rate of fire: 800-950 rpm
Magazine capacity: belt-fed
Users: Bolivia, Brunei, Chile

L4A4 Bren LMG light machine-gun

NEARLY SIX DECADES AFTER the first proto-type was completed at Enfield, and 70 years after the introduction of the original Czech design from which it was developed, the famous **Bren gun** is still in limited service with British forces.

The original Bren guns were based on the Czech **ZB 26**. Being magazine-fed, the Bren was not a true sustained-fire weapon, although it could be tripod-mounted, and with an effective and quick barrel change it could be used as such.

Originally chambered in .303-in calibre, existing Brens were converted in the 1950s when the British Army adopted the 7.62-mm x 45 NATO round as standard. This involved fitting new barrels, flash eliminators, ejectors, extractors and breech blocks. The most obvious difference lay in the straight magazine which replaced the original curved item.

The **L4A1** and **L4A2** were conversions of the original Bren Mk III, while the **L4A3** was based on the earlier Bren Mk II. Most guns still in service are

A South African machine-gunner fires a Bren re-chambered to accept 7.62-mm NATO ammunition. Note the straight magazine.

the **L4A4 LMG** model This is also a Mk III conversion, but with a chrome-lined bore for greatly extended barrel life.

The Bren is accurate, extremely reliable and immensely tough. It is still in use with British and Commonwealth armies, particularly with mobile forces, where its lighter weight gives it an advantage over heavier general-purpose machine-guns.

The original Bren, seen here alongside the L86 light support weapon intended as its replacement, is easily identifiable by its curved magazine, which was designed to hold British .303-inch (7.7-mm) rimmed rounds.

SPECIFICATION

Name: 7.62-mm L4A4 LMG
Type: light machine-gun
Calibre: 7.62-mm x 51 NATO
Weight: 8.68 kg
Dimensions: length 1156 mm; barrel length 597 mm
Muzzle velocity: 840 metres per second
Effective range: 800 m
Rate of fire: 520 rpm
Magazine capacity: 30-round box
Users: United Kingdom and many Commonwealth armies

Brens were milled from solid high-quality steel. Though expensive, the construction has contributed to the gun's longevity.

L7A2 GPMG general-purpose machine-gun

THE BRITISH ARMY'S **L7 General Purpose Machine-Gun** or **GPMG** is a development of the Belgian FN MAG, a superb weapon that has been adopted by armies all over the world. The British Army has used the GPMG for some 30 years. British guns are similar to other MAGs, but because of many small modifications to suit national manufacturing and operating practices, parts are not interchangeable.

There are a number of variants of the GPMG. The basic **L7A1** has a pistol grip and butt. The current standard **L7A2** has mounting points for attaching a 50-round belt box. The **L8A1** is a tank machine-gun, fitted with an electrical firing system and a bore evacuator to keep fumes out of the turret. The **L19** is a heavy-barrel version which has not been issued for service. The **L20** is a pod-mounted weapon intended to arm helicopters and light aircraft. The **L37** is a version for armoured

Known to generations of British soldiers as the 'Jimpy', the L7 GPMG has for more than three decades provided sterling service as a squad support weapon and in the sustained fire role.

vehicles, which has a folding pistol grip and can be fitted with a standard trigger, bipod and butt for dismounted use.

Before the introduction of the SA80 series of Individual weapons, each infantry section in the British Army included a gun group, centred around a GPMG, and a rifle group equipped with 7.62-mm SLRs. Theoretically replaced in the LMG role by the 5.56-mm LSW, the L7 was supposed to be used purely for sustained fire. But its great reliability and hard-hitting accuracy meant that many infantry units preferred the 'Jimpy' during the Gulf War. Whatever its theoretical advantages, the LSW is no substitute for a real machine-gun like the L7.

Unlike some GPMGs, the L7 can be carried safely cocked with an ammunition belt in place, ready for instant action.

SPECIFICATION
Name: 7.62-mm L7A2
Type: general-purpose machine-gun
Calibre: 7.62-mm x 51 NATO
Weight: 10.9 kg as LMG with bipod; 32 kg in sustained fire role with tripod, sighting unit and without butt
Dimensions: length with butt 1156 mm; barrel length 630 mm
Muzzle velocity: 838 metres per second
Effective range: 1500 m
Rate of fire: 750-1000 rpm
Magazine capacity: belt-fed
Users: United Kingdom and some Commonwealth armies

M2HB heavy machine-gun

IT IS A CURIOUS CHARACTERISTIC of the weapons used by modern armies that some of the most effective firearms in service are also some of the oldest. The Browning .50-calibre heavy machine-gun fired its first rounds more than 70 years ago, and over that long span it has remained one of the most fearsome infantry weapons on any battlefield.

The classic **M2** or **'Ma Deuce'** was developed from the original Browning **Model 1921** heavy machine-gun introduced not long after the end of World War I. In the 1930s, the design was simplified and a thicker barrel was fitted, hence the designation HB for Heavy Barrel. The **M2HB** has continued pretty much unchanged since then.

It has been built in a variety of models, all with similar mechanisms but with different barrels and mounts. Variants of the M2 have been mounted on jeeps, armoured vehicles, surface vessels, hovercraft, helicopters, and aircraft. But the standard

US Marines in the desert engage a target at long range with the hard-hitting 'Ma Deuce'. Armed with modern rounds, it is a fearsome anti-personnel weapon which can also be used to some effect against light armour, helicopters and aircraft.

M2HB is most widely used by infantryman against both ground and air targets.

The round is the heart of the weapon, and the big 'Fifty' is a prodigious man-stopper. It can penetrate vehicles, buildings and even light armoured vehicles. High-tech armour-piercing, incendiary and explosive rounds are continually being developed, adding to the weapon's already massive power.

Production of the M2 stopped in the 1970s, but in spite of numerous attempts to replace it troops in combat from the Falklands to the Gulf have found no substitute for the veteran's long-range punch. As a result the M2 is back in production in the USA and Belgium, and numerous improved versions are offered by a variety of manufacturers.

Unlike most modern machine-guns, the M2's trigger is a thumb-operated device which is pushed to fire.

SPECIFICATION

Name: M2HB
Type: heavy machine-gun
Calibre: .50-cal M2 ball (12.7-mm x 99)
Weight: 38 kg with tripod
Dimensions: length 1651 mm; barrel length 1143 mm
Muzzle velocity: 930 metres per second
Rate of fire: 450-600 rpm
Effective range: 2000 m
Magazine capacity: belt-fed
Users: United Kingdom, United States and at least 30 other countries around the world

M60 general-purpose machine-gun

THIS AMERICAN GENERAL-PURPOSE machine-gun appeared at much the same time as the FN MAG, but it proved to be an embarrassment from the start. Although many design features were copied from earlier, successful machine-guns like the German MG42, the **M60** was obviously inferior to the FN weapon and the Soviet PK.

The M60 was the standard US Army machine-gun throughout the Vietnam War, where its power was appreciated. However, its general awkwardness, particularly the need to wear asbestos gloves to change the barrel and permanently attached bipod, led it to be known as 'the Pig'. It has nevertheless been in service for three decades, although for the light role the US Army has replaced it with the 5.56-mm FN Minimi.

The Marine Corps has thoroughly redesigned the M60, and the resulting **M60E3** represents the best that can be achieved from a mediocre weapon. This lightweight version of the M60 has a new bipod

The M60's heyday was in Vietnam, where in spite of its faults it was a vital weapon both to infantry squads on patrol in the jungle and for arming vehicles and helicopters.

mounted on the receiver rather than on the barrel, and a new carrying handle attached to the barrel rather than the receiver. These allow hot barrels to be changed without the need for asbestos gloves. A forward pistol grip allows the gun to be used in the assault role. The M60E3 retains all the hard-hitting capabilities of the original gun in a package that is two kilograms lighter and far easier to use.

Incorporating operating and feed mechanisms copied from German weapons of World War II, the M60 is not as bad as its reputation, though it is expensive and the barrel change is clumsy.

SPECIFICATION

Name: M60
Type: general-purpose machine-gun
Calibre: 7.62-mm x 51 NATO
Weight: 11.1 kg; 17.9 kg with tripod; (M60E3 8.8 kg)
Dimensions: length 1105 mm; barrel length 560 mm
Muzzle velocity: 853 metres per second
Effective range: 1800 m (tripod); 1100m (bipod)
Rate of fire: 500-650 rpm
Magazine capacity: belt-fed
Users: Australia, United States, and at least 20 other countries around the world

The M60E3 introduced by the Marine Corps is a much improved weapon. Lighter and handier than the original, it has a better barrel change.

USSR
RPD light machine-gun

Although obsolete, the RPD remains a rugged and effective light machine-gun.

DESIGN OF THE **RPD** OR **DEGTYAREV** light machine-gun began at the height of World War II, when new ideas were coming to the fore about the shape and power of military small arms. Production began soon after Germany's surrender. The RPD was the first Soviet machine-gun designed to fire the new intermediate-power 7.62-mm x 39 cartridge, and was intended to partner the Kalashnikov assault rifle then coming into service.

In common with most post-war Soviet small arms, the RPD is a solid design, and was made in large numbers. A logical progression from the Degtyarev machine-gun of 1928, which as the **DPM** had been the standard Soviet LMG during World War II, it is a belt-fed weapon, generally feeding from a 100-round drum which clips to the bottom of the receiver. The RPD does not have a removable barrel so it is not suitable for sustained fire, but it is

an effective squad support weapon as long as the gunner fires in short bursts and does not exceed 100 rounds per minute.

It was also manufactured in China as the **Type 56** and **Type 56-1**, and the version built in North Korea was known as the **Type 62**. Used by most Soviet-supplied states, the RPD is now obsolete but can be found in armies all over Asia and Africa. The RPD has seen combat in wars ranging from the desert battles of the Middle East to the jungle struggles in Southeast Asia.

SPECIFICATION
Name: Ruchnoi Pulemyot Degtyareva
Type: light machine-gun
Calibre: 7.62-mm x 39
Weight: 7.1 kg
Dimensions: length 1036 mm; barrel length 521 mm
Muzzle velocity: 700 metres per second
Effective range: 700 m
Rate of fire: 700 rpm
Magazine capacity: belt-fed from 100-round drum
Users: China, Egypt, North Korea, Pakistan, Yemen; in reserve in former USSR, Warsaw Pact, and Soviet-influenced armies

---

USSR/RUSSIA
RPK squad support weapon

The RPK is an assault rifle with a longer, heavier barrel and a bipod, and shares many parts with the AKM. However, the length of the curved magazine makes it awkward to use from behind cover.

THE **RPK** IS A VARIANT of the famous Kalashnikov assault rifle fitted with a longer, heavier barrel. Because it lacks a barrel change and fires from magazines rather than belts, the RPK is not a sustained fire weapon. But like the British LSW (Light Support Weapon), it provides each infantry section with some extra firepower as well as a weapon that is more accurate at long range than a normal assault rifle. Generally fed from an AK-style 40-round magazine, it can also be equipped with a 75-round drum magazine.

Introduced in the mid-1960s, the RPK equips all former Soviet and ex-Warsaw Pact armies, as well as most Communist-backed guerrilla movements in the world. The **RPK-74** is a similar weapon which is

basically a long-barrelled version of the 5.45-mm x 39 calibre AK-74 assault rifle.

SPECIFICATION
Name: Ruchnoi Pulemyot Kalashnikova
Type: light machine-gun
Calibre: 7.62-mm x 39
Weight: 5.9 kg
Dimensions: length 1035 mm; barrel length 591 mm
Muzzle velocity: 732 metres per second
Effective range: 800 m
Rate of fire: 700 rpm
Magazine capacity: 40-round box or 75-round drum
Users: Russia, former Soviet Republics, Germany, former Warsaw Pact armies, and armies formerly under Soviet influence

The RPK is most often seen with a large 40-round banana-shaped AK rifle magazine.

PK general-purpose machine-gun

THE SOVIET **PK** MACHINE-GUN was introduced in 1964 and was soon supplied to Warsaw Pact allies and client states around the world. It was used by the North Vietnamese during the Vietnam War and has been seen in almost every guerrilla war for the last 25 years. Originally appearing in the light and assault machine-gun role, the PK has been applied to a variety of tasks so that it is now a true general-purpose machine-gun.

Designed as a company support weapon, the PK is a solid and reliable weapon in the FN MAG class which fires a full-power 7.62-mm round. Although dating back to the last century, the ballistic performance of the 7.62-mm cartridge is good. The only problem is that it has an old-style rimmed case, which can cause feed complications.

The basic infantry gun is either the PK or the

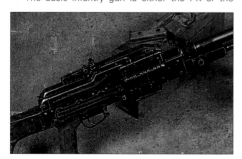

The PK uses a modified Kalashnikov operating system allied to an original feed mechanism.

Arms captured after the US invasion of Grenada included a large number of bipod-mounted PK general-purpose machine-guns.

PKS. The former is fitted with a bipod and the latter has a tripod mounting attachment. Incorporating features of a number of weapons, including the Kalashnikov, the RPD, and the Czech vz 52, it is still the standard infantry support machine-gun in ex-Warsaw Pact forces and in armies of former Soviet client states.

SPECIFICATION

Name: Pulemyot Kalashnikova
Type: general-purpose machine-gun
Calibre: 7.62-mm x 54 rimmed
Weight: 9 kg with bipod; 16.5 kg with tripod
Dimensions: length 1160 mm; barrel length 658 mm
Muzzle velocity: 825 metres per second
Effective range: 1000 m
Rate of fire: 690-720 rpm
Magazine capacity: 100-, 200- or 250-round belt
Users: Russia, former Soviet republics, former Warsaw Pact armies, and armies formerly under Soviet influence

The PK suffers little from recoil and has no tendency to climb when fired.

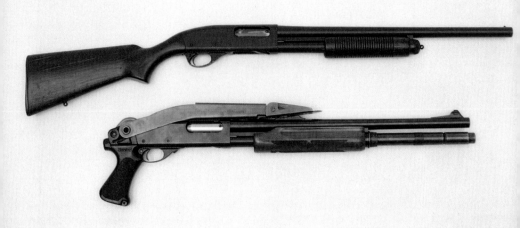

COMBAT SHOTGUNS

SPAS-12 combat shotgun

SHOTGUNS HAVE BEEN USED in combat for the best part of a century, but in general the weapons have been modified sporting guns. In the years since World War II, however, there has been considerable if intermittent interest in developing the shotgun specifically as a close-range assault weapon.

The **SPAS-12** was one of the first shotguns designed from the outset for military use. Luigi Franchi SpA had been working on the idea before the US Army decided they needed a close-range assault weapon; the American decision merely

Top: Unlike many shotguns used in combat, the SPAS 12 could not be mistaken for a sporting weapon. With its phosphated exterior and skeleton stock, it looks every inch a battlefield weapon.

Inset: The elbow hook on the skeleton stock allows the SPAS 12 to be fired one-handed.

added impetus to the Italian company's programme. And since 1979 the SPAS-12 has been the weapon to beat in the combat shotgun stakes.

With this gun Franchi introduced a host of innovations – semi-automatic or pump-action selectable at the press of a button, one-handed operation by using a special elbow hook on the folding stock, a shot diverter to give excellent lateral short-range spread, and a general air of combat efficiency which no shotgun ever had before. Somewhat bulky on first acquaintance, the SPAS-12 is a practical and efficient weapon.

The threatening aspect of the business end of the SPAS 12 is an intimidating weapon on its own.

SPECIFICATION

Name: SPAS 12
Type: selective-fire combat shotgun
Calibre: 12-gauge 2.75-inch (70-mm)
Weight: 4.2 kg
Dimensions: length 930 mm (710 mm with stock folded); barrel length 460 mm
Ammunition types: buckshot, solid slug, birdshot, plastic, CS gas, grenades
Effective range: shotshell 50-100 m; rifle grenades or solid slug 150-200m
Rate of fire: 250 rpm (theoretical); in practice 40 rpm
Magazine capacity: 7-round underbarrel tube
Users: Italy, police and special forces in many countries

RS 202 police/combat shotgun

The RS 202 M3 is a completely militarised version of Beretta's shotgun, with a detachable box magazine and pump- or semi-auto action.

ARMI BERETTA IS ONE OF the most respected names in the firearms business. Although well-known for its rifles and pistols, the firm also has a long tradition of shotgun manufacture. When the demand for military and paramilitary weapons began to mount, Beretta developed the conventional pump-action **RS 200P** military and police shotgun.

A conventional design with few innovations apart from a safety which prevented shells being fired unless the bolt was fully locked, the RS 200 was nevertheless built to the usual high Beretta standard. No longer in production, it was succeeded by the **RS 202P**, which is easier to load, and comes equipped with a folding stock. The **RS 202 M2** also has a perforated metal barrel guard, which eliminates the risks of burned hands from a hot barrel after repeated firing. It also has a variable choke device at the muzzle which allows the firer to control the spread of shot.

The **M3P** is a more thoroughly militarised weapon, which has a rifle-style magazine and, like the rival Franchi SPAS 12, can utilise both pump- and semi-auto action.

SPECIFICATION
Name: RS 202P
Type: pump-action combat shotgun
Calibre: 12-gauge 2.75-inch (70-mm)
Weight: 3.4 kg
Dimensions: length 1030 mm; barrel length 520 mm
Ammunition types: buckshot, solid slug, birdshot, CS gas
Effective range: shotshell 50-100 m; solid slug 100-150 m
Rate of fire: manual pump action
Magazine capacity: 6-round underbarrel tube
Users: several police forces

Striker close-assault/security weapon

The Striker is an extremely simple weapon, with very little to go wrong. Even so, its 12-round cylinder gives it awesome firepower.

DESIGNED IN SOUTH AFRICA by the Armsel company and, until the peaceful revolution in that country, marketed around the world by an Israeli licensee, the **Striker** is an ingenious design intended for use in a wide variety of situations.

A very simple and robust weapon, the main feature of the Striker is its 12-round rotary magazine, providing semi-automatic fire by means of a 'clockwork' magazine spring. Individual rounds are loaded through a trap on the right rear of the drum, and as the drum is turned the spring is tensioned. Once the weapon is loaded, each pull of the trigger fires a shot and rotates the next round into line. The barrel has a perforated metal sleeve, designed to protect the shooter's hands from hot barrels produced by extended periods of firing.

Although the company claims that it is suitable for civilian protection, it has found its main use in the hands of police forces. The 12-shot cylinder makes it rather bulky, but it is more comfortable to use than might be expected.

SPECIFICATION
Name: Striker
Type: semi-automatic revolving combat shotgun
Calibre: 12-gauge 2.75-inch (70-mm)
Weight: 3.4 kg empty; 4.20 kg loaded
Dimensions: length 780 mm (stock extended), 500 mm (folded); barrel length 300 mm
Ammunition types: buckshot, birdshot
Effective range: 75 m
Rate of fire: single-shot double action only
Magazine capacity: 12-round cylinder
Users: several police forces

USA
Remington 870 combat shotgun

US Marines train for riot duty with their Remington 870s. It is the shotgun's ability to fire non-lethal rounds like the gas grenades seen here which make it suitable for such tasks.

over the semi-automatic weapons then available.

The Model 870 has a seven-round tubular magazine, and can fire a wide variety of ammunition ranging from light shot and riot rounds to heavy buckshot and flechettes. Its primary function in Marine hands is for use in boarding parties, as a security weapon aboard ship, and as an embassy guard weapon with appropriate riot control munitions.

IN MANY WAYS THE UNITED STATES is the home of the combat shotgun. Used by the Marine Corps in the Philippines at the turn of the century, such weapons have seen action in most American wars since that time. And for the last three decades, the standard Marine Corps shotgun has been the **Remington Model 870**.

The Remington 870 is one of the most widely manufactured shotguns of all time, being produced in sporting and hunting versions as well as in dedicated police and security variants. When the US Marine Corps conducted trials to find a combat shotgun in the mid-1960s, it was decided that the reliability of the 870's pump action gave it the edge

SPECIFICATION
Name: Model 870 Mk 1
Type: pump-action combat shotgun
Calibre: 12-gauge 2.75-inch (70-mm)
Weight: 3.6 kg
Dimensions: length 1060 mm; barrel length 533 mm
Ammunition types: buckshot, birdshot, solid slug, flechette, CS, plastic baton, many others
Effective range: 50 m (shot), 400 m (flechette, in open country)
Rate of fire: single-shot manual pump action
Magazine capacity: 7-round tubular
Users: UK, USA, and armed and police forces all over the world

USA
Jackhammer close-assault weapon system

On full automatic, the Jackhammer can empty its magazine in just over two seconds. When empty, the 'cassette' is ejected and a new one slotted in.

constructed from an extremely tough new glass-reinforced plastic developed by Du Pont. The latest version of the design is the **Jackhammer Mk 3-A2**, with a recontoured buttstock for better recoil characteristics and numerous detail improvements.

The Jackhammer is stronger than a normal shotgun, and can fire a special round known as a 'Jack Shot'. This can carry double the payload of conventional shotgun rounds, and can fire at much greater pressures. In addition, the ammunition cassette can be detached and used as an anti-personnel mine.

THE **JACKHAMMER** HAS BEEN under development by the Pancor Corporation of New Mexico for many years. Like other high-capacity weapons of the type, it has a revolving magazine, but with some differences, not the least of which is its space-age appearance.

The Jackhammer is an advanced 'Bullpup' design, with the magazine behind the trigger group. The cylinder is completely removable and is not reloaded; it is merely dropped out when fired and replaced with a new loaded 'ammo cassette'. The circumference of the magazine is grooved rather like the old Webley-Fosbery revolver. Gas extracted from the barrel drives a piston, a stud on the piston engaging the groove and driving the cylinder around. It will fire full-automatic at 240 rounds per minute.

The barrel, return spring and actuating rod which turns the cylinder are all manufactured from high-quality steel. Most of the rest of the weapon is

SPECIFICATION
Name: Jackhammer Mk 3-A2
Type: automatic combat shotgun
Calibre: 12-gauge 2.75-inch (70-mm)
Weight: 4.57 kg
Dimensions: length 787 mm; barrel 525 mm
Ammunition types: buckshot, birdshot, anti-armour, flechette, explosive/shrapnel, canister, chemical, rocket-assisted
Effective range: 150 m
Rate of fire: 240 rpm (cyclic)
Magazine capacity: 12-round cylinder
Users: prototype development

AS-3 close-assault weapon system

Built and handled like an assault rifle, the AS offers much more accuracy and versatility than previous combat shotgun types.

10-shot box magazine, which is designed to handle the wide variety of advanced ammunition developed for the CAWS programme as well as standard 12-gauge shot or slug rounds.

The weapon is built from massive alloy forgings and plastic. The long barrel makes it very accurate, and the three-round burst is rather more practical than the full-automatic option. The barrel is fitted with a large compensator to ease controllability in full automatic fire.

THE US ARMY'S INTEREST in advanced shot-guns formed part of the Joint Service Small Arms Program of the 1970s and 1980s. One component was the Close Assault Weapon System, or CAWS, for which the **Smith & Wesson Assault Shotgun (AS)** was produced.

Although better known for its pistols, the Smith & Wesson concern has long been a manufacturer of shotguns, largely for police use. But the AS is a con-siderably more advanced military system. Designed along the lines of an assault rifle, the AS has been built as the **AS-1** in single-shot semi-auto, the **AS-2** in semi-auto plus a three-round burst, and as the full-auto-capable **AS-3**. This last version can fire at a cyclic rate of 375 rounds a minute. Feed is from a

SPECIFICATION

Name: AS-3
Type: automatic combat shotgun
Calibre: 12-gauge 2.75-inch (70-mm) or 3-inch Magnum
Weight: 5.69 kg loaded
Dimensions: length 1054 mm; barrel length 476 mm
Ammunition types: armour penetrator, flechette, explosive/shrapnel, buckshot, birdshot, canister, liquid or solid chemical, rocket-assisted projectiles
Effective range: 100 m
Rate of fire: 375 rpm (cyclic)
Magazine capacity: 10-round box
Users: development; ready for manufacture

Olin/HK CAWS close-assault weapon system

The CAWS bears a family resemblance to H&K's revolutionary G11 rifle, although it is made largely of steel rather than plastic.

Close Assault Weapon System. More akin to modern assault rifles than to previous shotgun designs, the CAWS is a recoil-operated semi-auto or full-auto weapon, with significantly less 'kick' than previous weapons of this type.

It is a fighting weapon pure and simple, fed from a box magazine located behind the trigger, with an optical sight set in the carrying handle over the body. This is an unusual feature in a shotgun, and gives an indication as to the kind of range at which the weapon is expected to be effective.

THE US JOINT SERVICES SMALL ARMS PROGRAM decided in 1979 that there was a requirement for a RHINO (Repeating Hand-held Improved Non-rifled Ordnance). In short, what was required was an improved shotgun with no restraints placed on design other than the amount of felt recoil.

The Winchester ammunition group of Olin Industries started the ball rolling by designing a shell with hit probability and penetration that was signifi-cantly better than existing shotgun rounds, and then developed a three-inch brass-belted round capable of firing conventional ball bearing or flechettes out to 150 metres. Standard payload is eight tungsten alloy pellets capable of penetrating a 20-mm pine board or 1.5-mm of steel plate at a range of 150 m.

The weapon was then designed around the cartridge by Heckler & Koch and named **CAWS** for

SPECIFICATION

Name: Close Assault Weapon System
Type: automatic combat shotgun
Calibre: 12-gauge 3-inch (76-mm) CAWS
Weight: 4.08 kg (empty)
Dimensions: length 762 mm; barrel length 457 mm
Ammunition types: armour penetrator, flechette, explosive/shrapnel, buckshot, birdshot, canister, liquid or solid chemical, rocket-assisted projectiles
Effective range: 150 m
Rate of fire: 200-300 rpm (cyclic)
Magazine capacity: 10-round box
Users: prototype development

SILENCED WEAPONS

9-mm Suppressed AUG suppressed sub-machine gun

The silenced AUG is currently in service with Austrian special forces units, and may also be used by other operators of the AUG system.

gun version of the AUG, since its relatively low-power rounds are easier to muffle than the high-velocity 5.56-mm rounds used in the assault rifle.

The suppressed AUG's bullpup configuration allows it to be fitted with a 420-mm barrel, promising considerable accuracy in a conveniently short weapon. It is fitted with a standard x1.5 optical sight and can produce 125-mm groups at 100 metres. Specialised subsonic ammunition is also available, making the weapon even quieter to fire.

STEYR-MANNLICHER OFFERS a version of its best-selling **AUG** rifle fitted with a suppressor. It is not a truly silenced weapon: the suppressor reduces the velocity of the propellant gases to subsonic speed so there is no loud muzzle report. However, bullet velocity is not reduced, so the characteristic 'crack' – the sound wave generated by rounds passing supersonically through the air – is still present.

The weapon is based on the 9-mm sub-machine

SPECIFICATION
Name: Armee Universal Gewehr
Calibre: 9-mm x 19 Parabellum
Weight: 3.3 kg empty
Dimensions: length 785 mm (including typical suppressor); barrel length 420 mm
Muzzle velocity: 400 metres per second
Effective range: 200 m
Rate of fire: 650/750 rpm (cyclic)
Magazine capacity: 25- or 32-round box
Users: Austrian special forces

The silenced AUG is based on the standard AUG machine pistol.

Type 64 sub-machine gun silenced sub-machine gun

The Type 64 is a purpose-built gun designed for clandestine operations by special forces units.

of the century. The pistol cartridge is not particularly powerful, so a Chinese assassin needs to be close to his target and able to place his shots very accurately. The barrel only extends to about half the length of the suppressor, and the last part of it is perforated by series of holes. The front part of the silencer consists of a series of baffles which extend to the muzzle. In addition to cutting down the sound of a shot being fired, it also acts as a flash hider.

MOST SILENCED GUNS are conventional weapons fitted with suppressors, generally conversions of existing designs. The **Type 64 sub-machine gun** was designed from the outset for use by special forces and and clandestine units.

The design is an interesting combination: the bolt action is a copy of that on the Soviet PPS-43, the trigger copies that of the Bren gun – or rather the mechanism follows the design of pre-war Czech ZB series of machine-guns bought by the Nationalists in the 1930s.

The Type 64 is a simple blowback weapon. It fires the standard Chinese 7.62-mm x 25 pistol cartridge, adapted from the Soviet World War II pistol and sub-machine gun round which itself was copied from the 7.63-mm Mauser round of the turn

SPECIFICATION
Name: Type 64
Calibre: 7.62-mm x 25
Weight: 3.4 kg
Dimensions: length 843 mm with stock extended; barrel length 244 mm
Muzzle velocity: 513 metres per second
Effective range: 140 m
Rate of fire: 1315 rpm (cyclic)
Magazine capacity: 30-round box
Users: China

FINLAND
Vaime SSR MK 2 silenced rifle

Based on the action of the Finnish army's standard sniping rifle, the Vaime uses an integral suppressed barrel to reduce noise.

FINLAND'S OY VAIMENNINMETALLI AB specialises in producing suppressors and silenced weapons for hunting and military use. The company produces a range of add-on suppressors for use with military rifles and pistols of up to 11.6-mm calibre, as well as for sporting rifles and for small-calibre high-velocity 'varmint' weapons.

The **Vaime SSR Mk 2** or **Super Silenced Rifle** is a purpose-built sniper's weapon suitable for both military special forces and police special tactics use. Based on a standard bolt-action manufactured by Sako, which builds the Finnish army's sniper rifles, it is mated to an integrally silenced barrel, a non-reflective plastic stock and an articulated bipod. The Mk 2 is intended to fire special subsonic 7.62-mm x 51 ammunition with a muzzle velocity of 320 metres per second.

The result is a spectacularly silent weapon, with little or no felt recoil on firing. Unfortunately, the low-power ammunition means a highly curved trajectory and limited range, so a sniper has to get within 200 metres of his target to be sure of a kill. In emergencies the Mk 2 can fire 7.62-mm NATO without suffering any harm, but since the silencer does not slow the round to subsonic speeds the bullet will create a loud crack as it travels.

Vaime also offers a similar rifle chambered for .22LR for training purposes. Known as the **Mk 3**, it is also suitable for special forces missions or for urban operations, where over-penetration and the risk of harming bystanders by using full-power ammunition could be a serious problem.

SPECIFICATION
Name: SSR (Super Silenced Rifle)
Calibre: 7.62-mm x 51 NATO; subsonic rounds used for maximum silenced effect
Weight: 4.1 kg
Dimensions: length 1180 mm; barrel length 720 mm
Muzzle velocity: under 320 metres per second when using subsonic ammunition
Effective range: 200 m
Rate of fire: single-shot, manual bolt action
Magazine capacity: 5 rounds
Users: not revealed

GERMANY
MP5 SD silenced sub-machine gun

The MP5 SD3 has a sliding metal stock. Later versions have a three-round burst control.

THE MP5 SUB-MACHINE GUN manufactured by the German firm of Heckler & Koch is one of the great success stories in post-war firearms manufacture. It is more complicated than many of its contemporaries, but at the same time is more accurate. It is this accuracy which has made it all but standard equipment with special operations forces around the world.

The **MP5 SD** is the silenced version of the MP5, which uses the normal Heckler & Koch roller locking mechanism. It fires through a barrel drilled with 30 holes only 3 mm in diameter, around which a suppressor is fitted. The silencer reduces the muzzle velocity with standard 9-mm ammunition to subsonic speed, doing away with the need for specially loaded ammunition. The muzzle report sounds rather like the airbrake on a lorry: you can hear it up to 100 metres away but it is not recognisable as a gunshot unless you fire bursts. Single-shot accuracy is excellent within 100 metres and the silencer requires no special maintenance, just rinsing with a cleaning agent after use.

As with all of the MP5 range, the SD is offered in a variety of forms and specifications. It is available with no butt as the **SD1**, with a fixed butt as the **SD2** and with a sliding stock as the **SD3**. The same weapons with three-round burst control are designated **SD4**, **SD5** and **SD6** respectively. All can be used with telescopic, night or laser sights.

SPECIFICATION
Name: MP5 SD
Calibre: 9-mm x 19 Parabellum
Weight: SD1 2.9 kg; SD2 3.2 kg; SD3 3.5 kg
Dimensions: 680 mm, 490 mm butt retracted; barrel length 146 mm
Muzzle velocity: 285 metres per second
Effective range: 150 m
Rate of fire: 800 rpm cyclic
Magazine capacity: 15- or 30-round box
Users: special operations units all over the world, including Germany, United Kingdom and the USA

UNITED KINGDOM
De Lisle carbine silenced commando weapon

The De Lisle's multi-baffle silencer is one of the most effective ever developed.

SILENCED AND SUPPRESSED firearms have been around since the end of the 19th century, one of the first designs for just such a weapon having come from the fertile brain of Hiram Maxim. But it was during World War II with the evolution of a whole new method of clandestine warfare that demand for such weapons took off.

The **De Lisle carbine** was one of the earliest and best of such weapons. Possibly the quietest firearm ever produced, it is accurate to at least 250 metres, outranging almost all silenced sub-machine guns and many silenced rifles.

Developed for British commandos, it combines the action of the Lee-Enfield rifle with the .45 ACP pistol cartridge. The large silencer is almost completely effective, and the heavy bullet is an accurate round. The only drawback to the De Lisle is that, being bolt-action, a second shot requires you to work the bolt to chamber the next round, which makes far more noise than firing! But for the one-shot, silent headshot at over 100 metres, the De Lisle was unbeatable.

Few of these highly effective weapons now remain intact, most having been destroyed by the authorities after the end of World War II. This was designed to prevent their falling into the wrong hands for use as assassination weapons.

SPECIFICATION
Name: De Lisle carbine
Calibre: .45 ACP
Weight: 3.74 kg
Dimensions: length 894 mm; barrel length 184 mm
Muzzle velocity: 253 metres per second
Effective range: 250 m
Rate of fire: single-shot bolt-action
Magazine capacity: 7-round box
Users: British Army

UNITED KINGDOM
L34A1 Sterling SMG silenced commando weapon

Marine Commandos armed with L34s come ashore. Silenced Sterling sub-machine guns have used by British special forces for many years.

ALTHOUGH ITS DESIGN DATES BACK to the 1940s, the **Sterling** sub-machine gun is one of the most rugged and dependable weapons of its type. Built to a very high standard, it is also available with an integral silencer.

The silenced version is given the designation **L34A1** by the British Army and the Royal Marines. It has been issued to special forces and raiding units, and is also used by a number of Commonwealth and Middle Eastern armies, while single-shot versions are used by police forces in the British Isles.

The L34 fires the same 9-mm Parabellum ammunition as the standard L2A3 sub-machine gun. It has 72 small holes drilled in the barrel, which disperse some of the the propellant gases into a diffuser tube, which is enclosed in its turn by a metal wrap. This has the double effect of slowing the bullet and reducing muzzle report. The silencer itself extends forwards from the end of the barrel. Mechanical noise is inaudible at 30 metres, and the sound cannot be recognised as a gunshot at 50 metres.

SPECIFICATION
Name: L34A1 sub-machine gun
Calibre: 9-mm x 19 Parabellum
Weight: 3.6 kg (empty)
Dimensions: length 864 mm (stock extended); barrel length 198 mm
Muzzle velocity: 293-310 metres per second
Effective range: 150 m
Rate of fire: 515-565 rpm (cyclic)
Magazine capacity: 7-round box
Users: British Army and police forces, Commonwealth armies and some Gulf states

Silenced pistols

RIFLES AND LONG ARMS are not the only weapons which use silencers. Hollywood-style silenced pistols also have a place in military affairs, especially for clandestine work. They are smaller and more unobtrusive than sub-machine guns or rifles, and are much more easy to hide. Although they fire less powerful rounds which lack range, they make less noise in the first place, and are much simpler to suppress. Small-calibre and low-power rounds are also more useful at close quarters, where pinpoint accuracy does away with the need for stopping power or long-range performance.

Silenced pistols come in a variety of shapes and sizes. Some are standard guns to which a suppressor is added, and range in type from pre-war designs such as the Walther P38 to the latest high-tech composite-construction wonders. Add-on suppressors can be very effective, but they can never match suppressors built in to the design. And in the clandestine world the ultimate silenced weapons are often variants of .22-calibre target pistols

Weapons like the High Standard or the Ruger Mk II .22LR target pistol are popular choices, being accurate and robust. The round may not be the most powerful, but at close range a head shot is just as

This Swiss-built development of the CZ75 is typical of many modern pistols in being able to accept a large sound suppressor.

Inset: The huge suppressor fitted to this Walther P38 screws onto the specially threaded barrel.

lethal as one from a larger-calibre gun.

Such silenced pistols are used by groups as diverse as local pest-control officers, the US Navy SEALs and Israel's Mossad secret intelligence service. The latest versions are almost completely noiseless and are accurate to 70 metres and more.

SPECIFICATION

Name: Ruger Mk II
Cartridge: .22LR
Weight: 1.43 kg
Dimensions: length 342 mm; barrel length 175 mm
Muzzle velocity: 246 m/sec (with standard ammunition); 194 m/sec (with subsonic ammunition)
Effective range: 0-70 metres
Rate of fire: semi-automatic single shot
Magazine: 9-round box
Users: US Army and US Navy special forces; special forces and clandestine units in Europe, the Middle East and Asia

GRENADE-LAUNCHERS

GERMANY
40-mm **Granatpistole** grenade-launcher

The Granatpistole is a modern, highly effective close-range infantry support and riot-control weapon.

HECKLER & KOCH HAS sold the **Granatpistole**, a single-shot break-action grenade-launcher, to the German army and several other military and paramilitary organisations.

The Granatpistole has a retractable butt, collapsing to a very handy 463 mm, with fold-down sights as well. A wide variety of grenades and riot-control munitions can be launched with or without the stock extended.

Equipped with a folding 'ladder' type of rear sight, the Granatpistole effectively fills the gap between hand-thrown grenades and minimum mortar range. By using the fixed sights presented when the main sight is lowered, the weapon can fire directly on an almost flat trajectory out to a range of around 100 metres. Delivering grenades to any

greater distances out to a maximum of 350 metres or more calls for high-angle fire, which requires that the rear sights be flipped up for maximum accuracy.

The Granatpistole barrel pivots when the cocking handle is fully withdrawn, permitting a fresh cartridge to be loaded. Spent cases are extracted manually.

Heckler & Koch also makes the **HK79**, a weapon for attaching direct to rifles, which fits on most full-sized H&K rifles. Both grenade-launchers can fire the huge range of US 40-mm grenades.

SPECIFICATION
Name: Granatpistole
Calibre: 40 mm
Dimensions: length 683 mm (stock extended); barrel length 356 mm
Weight: 2.3 kg
Muzzle velocity: 75 metres per second
Ammunition: full range of standard NATO lethal and non-lethal 40-mm projectiles
Range: 350 m
Users: German army and police and a number of forces worldwide

---

SINGAPORE
CIS 40GL grenade-launcher

Similar in concept to the American M203, the CIS 40GL is fitted with sights calibrated to 350 metres.

launcher, it can be fired independently or attached to most service rifles. A single-shot breech-loading weapon, the CIS 40 is of modular construction. It consists of just four assemblies: receiver, barrel, leaf sight and buttstock or rifle adaptor. This helps ensure reliability as well as simplicity of manufacture and maintenance.

The weapon is loaded by depressing the charging lever on the left-hand side of the receiver, automatically unlocking the barrel, cocking the firing pin and applying the safety catch. The barrel swings out for easy loading and is swung back manually ready for launch.

The folding leaf sight can be adjusted both in elevation for range and in azimuth to allow for wind. It is graduated in 50-metre increments to 350 metres.

OVER THE PAST TWO DECADES the island republic of Singapore has developed a significant arms industry, manufacturing weapons from small arms to fighting ships. Chartered Firearms Industries manufactures a wide range of infantry weapons, including the **CIS 40GL**, a very competitive 40-mm grenade-launcher.

A shoulder-fired multi-purpose grenade-

SPECIFICATION
Name: CIS 40GL
Calibre: 40 mm
Dimensions: length 655 mm; barrel length 305 mm
Weight: 2.05 kg (loaded)
Muzzle velocity: 71 metres per second
Ammunition: full range of standard 40-mm ammunition
Range: 400 m
Users: in production for a number of undisclosed countries

M203 40-mm grenade-launcher grenade-launcher

DEVELOPED BY THE AAI CORPORATION in the late 1960s and manufactured by Colt, the **M203** replaced the M79 in the US armed forces during the 1970s. The problem with previous weapons was that to carry a dedicated grenade-launcher meant that an infantry squad had to sacrifice one of its rifles. Fitted underneath an M16 rifle, the M203 provided grenade-launching capability without any loss of firepower.

A single-shot breech-loader, the M203 is worked like a pump-action shotgun and is able to deliver grenades with reasonable accuracy to more than twice the effective range of an M79. The 1970s version could only be fitted to M16 rifles, but there is now a 'product-improved' M203 that is mounted

The M203 was introduced at the end of the Vietnam War, and was one of the first grenade-launchers designed either to be mounted under the barrel of an assault rifle or to be used as a weapon in its own right.

on an interbar which can be clipped to almost any service rifle.

The M203 can also be fitted with a 'snap-on' folding stock/pistol grip for use on its own as a light, effective infantry-support weapon.

The M203 operates like a large-calibre single-shot pump-action shotgun. It can be fitted with a folding butt and pistol grip for independent use.

SPECIFICATION

Name: M203
Calibre: 40-mm
Dimensions: length 380 mm; barrel length 305 mm
Weight: 1.63 kg (loaded)
Muzzle velocity: 75 metres per second
Ammunition: full range of standard 40-mm ammunition
Range: 400 m
Users: United States armed forces, many US police forces, most NATO armed forces

The product-improved version of the M203 incorporates a mounting rail over the top of the weapon which can clip under the barrel of most modern assault rifles.

USA
M79 grenade-launcher grenade-launcher

An M79 gunner guarding the perimeter of a firebase on the outskirts of Saigon at the height of the Vietnam War loads a non-lethal CS gas cartridge into his M79.

several South American and Asian nations, and is still manufactured in Korea.

SPECIFICATION
Name: M79
Calibre: 40 mm
Dimensions: length 737 mm; barrel length 356 mm
Weight: 2.95 kg (loaded)
Muzzle velocity: 76 metres per second
Ammunition: more than 20 types from the USA alone, including HE, multiple projectile, flechette, illumination, smoke, riot control and CS gas
Range: 350 m (area targets) or 150 m (point targets)
Users: Korea and several Asian and South American countries

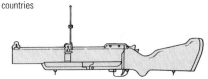

The 'bloop gun' breaks open at the breech and loads like a short, stubby shotgun. It was the first weapon designed to fire the spin-stabilised 40-mm grenades which are now standard infantry weapons.

THE **M79** IS A SINGLE-SHOT BREECH-LOADING weapon developed for the US Army during the 1950s, which entered service in 1961. More than 350,000 were manufactured, and it was extensively used in Vietnam, where it was known as the 'bloop gun'. It was replaced by the M203, since a soldier equipped with an M79 could not carry a rifle as well.

The spin-stabilised 40-mm ammunition designed for the M79 was highly influential, with most modern free world grenade-launchers being designed to fire it. The M79 is capable of surprising accuracy in trained hands, in spite of its incredibly high trajectory. Although replaced in US service, the M79 was exported widely and remains in use with

USA
RAW assault support weapon

The RAW's large spherical warhead carries a much more powerful explosive charge than standard grenades, and its rocket motor propels it much faster.

than 300 mm across in 200-mm thick reinforced concrete. This is far in excess of the capability of standard 40-mm grenades, and not far short of what can be achieved by artillery rounds.

However, the RAW is a bulky weapon by comparison with standard 40-mm grenades. Although its internal rocket will propel the projectile to a maximum range of 2000 metres, engagement ranges in urban terrain are invariably much shorter, and the RAW's effective range is about 300 metres.

THE **RAW** (RIFLEMAN'S ASSAULT WEAPON) originates in a US Army and US Marine requirement for a powerful short-range man-portable urban combat weapon capable of dealing with enemy strongpoints protected by sandbags or even concrete pillboxes.

The RAW is a novel device which is fitted to the underside of the muzzle of a standard M16 rifle. Propellant gases emerging from the muzzle from firing an ordinary rifle round are bled off. Channelled down a tube, the gases drive the RAW's firing pin forward, which ignites a cap which in turn sets off the projectile's rocket motor.

The spin-stabilised spherical rocket-powered projectile contains one kilogram of high explosive that 'pancakes' on striking the target, producing a spectacular effect against concrete structures or light armoured vehicles. It can blow a hole more

SPECIFICATION
Name: RAW
Calibre: 140 mm
Dimensions: length 305 mm
Weight: 4.73 kg (clip-on launcher with 1-kg projectile)
Projectile velocity: 175 metres per second at 200 m
Ammunition: HE squash head, HE fragmentation, anti-armour, smoke, incendiary and chemical
Range: 2000 m (area targets); 300 m (individual targets)
User: USA

Mk 19 40-mm automatic grenade-launcher

The Mk 19 can be mounted on light special forces vehicles, where it provides what amounts to light artillery support.

used with day, night and laser sights. It is an air-cooled, blowback-operated machine-gun that fires belted ammunition from an open bolt. The disintegrating link belt is unusual in that each link stays with the cartridge and is ejected with it.

THE **MK 19** IS DESIGNATED as a machine-gun, but is in fact an automatic belt-fed grenade-launcher. It was developed for the US Navy as an attempt to provide small river patrol craft a light-weight source of real firepower. Entering service in Vietnam in 1967, it fired similar grenades to the contemporary M79 but at much higher velocity. Soon acquired by the US and Israeli armies, it had some reliability problems and an improved model was introduced in the early 1970s, while the current **Mk 19 Mod 3**, which entered production in the 1980s, is a greatly simplified weapon which is much easier and much less costly to manufacture .

The Mk 19 is effective against personnel and light armour. Tripod-mounted by infantry, it can also be mounted on vehicles or in turrets, and can be

SPECIFICATION
Name: Mk 19 Mod 3
Calibre: 40 mm
Dimensions: length 1028 mm; height 206 mm
Weight: 34 kg
Muzzle velocity: 240 metres per second
Ammunition: HE, practice
Rate of fire: 325-375 rpm
Range: 1600 m
Users: numerous forces including Ecuador, Honduras, Israel, United Kingdom and USA

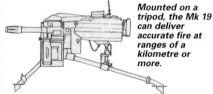

Mounted on a tripod, the Mk 19 can deliver accurate fire at ranges of a kilometre or more.

AGS-17 automatic grenade-launcher

In service for more than two decades, the infantry version of the AGS-17 was never exported and now serves only with former Soviet states.

The AGS-17 is smaller in calibre than the American Mk 19, and does not have as high a rate of fire. Blowback-operated, it is belt-fed from the right and ejects the empty cases through the bottom of the chamber. Ammunition belts are usually supplied in protective drums which hold up to 29 rounds and which clip directly onto the receiver.

Its exceptional range means that the AGS-17 has a much higher response potential than a mortar, and its ability to fire automatically means that it is not handicapped by the relatively small size of its standard 30-mm grenades.

FIRST INTRODUCED BY THE SOVIET army in the mid-1970s, the **AGS-17 Plamya** ('Flame') is a 30-mm grenade-launcher which was issued to the infantry companies of Motor Rifle regiments in sections of two. Like the American Mk 19, which it resembles, the AGS-17 can be mounted in a number of ways. Normally seen on a tripod, it has been fitted to assault helicopters and has also been seen on BTR-70 APCs.

Extensively used in Afghanistan, where its high elevation enabled it to engage guerrillas firing down from the mountain peaks, the AGS-17 also became part of the Mujahideen armoury as some of them were captured.

SPECIFICATION
Name: Automatichesky Granatomat Stankovy
Calibre: 30 mm
Dimensions: length 840 mm; barrel length 290 mm
Weight: 18 kg; 52 kg with tripod
Muzzle velocity: probably up to 200 metres per second
Ammunition: HE, fragmentation, practice
Rate of fire: 65 rpm
Effective range: 1200m (1750m max)
Users: Russia and former Soviet armies

MORTARS

L16 81-mm infantry mortar

THE CLASSIC INFANTRYMAN'S mortar is between 75 and 85 mm in calibre – small enough to be carried by troops on foot, yet large enough to fire a decent bomb. The 81-mm **L16** is the British Army's standard mortar of this type. It is designed to fire most NATO standard 81-mm rounds which are used throughout the world, as well as British HE, smoke, practice and illumination bombs. A new guided round called Merlin has a tiny radar seeker in the nose and also gives a precision attack capability against tanks and point targets.

One of the reasons that the L16 has been such a success is its sturdiness and the ability to sustain fire for long periods, even when using powerful propellant charges which on other weapons would make the mortar too hot to handle. The L16's barrel is thicker than that of many similar weapons, and it is fitted with cooling fins to help dissipate the heat generated by rapid firing.

The baseplate is a Canadian design. Made from forged aluminium, it allows the mortar to be traversed through 360 degrees. The sight is also Canadian, and can be used on both mortars and on sustained fire GPMGs.

Widely exported and even in service with the US Army, the L16 is man-portable with a three-man crew. It provided vital fire support during the Falklands war when British forces were desperately short of artillery. The L16 performs so well that the British Army no longer uses heavy mortars, preferring the hail of fire that is possible from the L16. It also provides mobile firepower; mechanised battalions carry and fire the L16 from converted FV 432 personnel carriers.

A British Army mortar team provides supporting fire as an infantry attack goes in. Mortars like the L16 can be likened to lightweight, portable artillery, allowing foot soldiers to attack an enemy with high explosive well beyond rifle range.

SPECIFICATION

Name: L16 ML
Calibre: 81-mm
Barrel length: 1280 mm
Weight: 36.6 kg (barrel 12.7 kg, mounting 12.3 kg, baseplate 11.6 kg)
Weight of bomb: 4.2 kg
Types of bomb: high-explosive, illuminating, smoke, practice, and guided anti-armour
Rate of fire: 15 rpm sustained
Minimum range: 100 m
Maximum range: 5650 m
Users: Austria, Bahrain, Canada, Guyana, India, Kenya, Malawi, Malaysia, New Zealand, Nigeria, Norway, Oman, Qatar, United Arab Emirates, UK, USA, Yemen

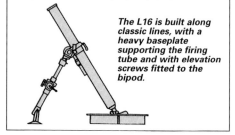

The L16 is built along classic lines, with a heavy baseplate supporting the firing tube and with elevation screws fitted to the bipod.

USA

M224 60-mm light mortar

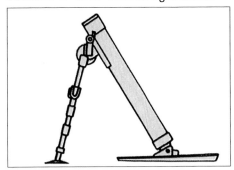

Light mortars are easy to carry and deploy, and are invaluable to infantry units fighting far from support or the chance of resupply.

lost on the US Army, and in 1970 development of a new weapon began. In 1977 the **M224 lightweight company mortar** was introduced for infantry and airborne forces. Intended to produce a high volume of fire at either high or low angles, the M224 can be fired with or without a bipod and uses special multi-fuse ammunition, equipped with an M734 fuse offering the choice of high or low airburst and detonation on contact or delayed detonation.

ALTHOUGH 81-MM MORTARS are highly effective in static fire bases, carrying them and their ammunition in difficult terrain demands a great deal of manpower. Some US infantry companies in action in Vietnam's jungles reverted to using the obsolete **M19** or even the pre-war **M2** 60-mm mortar. They were much lighter and handier, and troops on foot could carry a great deal more ammunition. The M19 is a simple muzzle-loading weapon but is trigger-fired. It was widely exported to Asia and South America, and was licence-manufactured in Belgium and Canada.

The lessons learned in Southeast Asia were not

SPECIFICATION
Name: M224
Calibre: 60 mm
Barrel length: 1073 mm
Weight: hand-held with light baseplate 7.8 kg; 19 kg with standard baseplate and bipod
Weight of bomb: 2.26 kg
Types of bomb: HE, illuminating, smoke, and practice
Rate of fire: 30 rpm burst; 18 rpm for four minutes; 10 rpm sustained
Minimum range: 375 m (illumination); 90 m (smoke); 45 m (high explosive and practice)
Maximum range: 1500 m
User: USA

USA

M30 107-mm heavy mortar

The M30 has been in service for many years, and though long out of production remains the standard US Army heavy mortar.

SPECIFICATION
Name: M30
Calibre: 107.7-mm (4.2 inch)
Barrel length: 1524 mm
Weight: 305 kg fully assembled
Weight of bomb: 10-12.98 kg
Types of bomb: HE, smoke, illumination, CS gas, chemical
Rate of fire: 18 rpm burst, 9 rpm for five minutes, then 3-4 rpm sustained
Minimum range: 770 m (HE); 400 m (illumination)
Maximum range: 6800 m (HE); 4620 m (smoke)
Users: USA, Austria, Belgium, Canada, Greece, Iran, Netherlands, Norway, Oman, S.Korea, Turkey, Zaïre

The M30 is not the most portable of weapons, its main components weighing in at a hefty 305 kg. But its larger size means that it can fire heavyweight bombs to match.

UNLIKE THE BRITISH, the US Army has retained heavy mortars. Weighing more than 300 kilograms in action, they are too heavy to be manhandled with ease and are usually mounted in armoured personnel carriers or fired from fixed positions.

Although far from mobile, the 107-mm M30, which was used extensively in Vietnam, can be disassembled into five parts to allow short-distance manhandling, although most of the parts need two men to lift them. A muzzle-loading drop-fired weapon, the **M30** is unusual in that its barrel is rifled. Its rounds are semi-fixed; stabilised in flight by spinning, like an artillery round, they do not need tailfins as used on other mortar bombs.

USSR/RUSSIA
M43 160-mm heavy mortar

Although more like an artillery piece than an infantry weapon, the Soviets used this huge mortar to provide fire support to soldiers on foot.

SOVIET MILITARY PLANNERS were great believers in the mortar, and the Red Army was the greatest user of these weapons in the world. Mortars were sturdy, reliable and cheap to manufacture, and they were also simple to operate. Soviet mortars ranged from small hand-held infantry weapons to self-propelled monsters as big as artillery pieces which were capable of firing nuclear bombs.

The **M1943** was the heaviest mortar employed by Soviet forces during World War II. It was widely exported to Warsaw Pact armies during the 1950s, and since it was effective and reliable it has remained in service to this day.

A larger modernised version, the **M-160**, was introduced in 1953 and is still in the inventories of former Soviet states. The Indian Army used them in 1971, and they have also been in action in most Arab-Israeli conflicts.

A giant 240-mm mortar was also produced in 1952, with an improved self-propelled version entering service in 1980. The latter has an automatic loading system.

SPECIFICATION
Name: M43
Calibre: 160-mm
Barrel length: 3030 mm (M-160 4550 mm)
Weight: 1170 kg (M-160 1300 kg)
Weight of bomb: 41 kg
Types of bomb: high-explosive, HE fragmentation, smoke, illumination; probably chemical
Rate of fire: 3-4 rpm sustained
Minimum range: 630 metres
Maximum range: 5150 m (M-160 8000m)
Users: former Soviet republics, Albania, China, Czech Republic, Egypt, Germany, North Korea, Slovakia, Vietnam

---

USSR/RUSSIA
M-37 82-mm light mortar

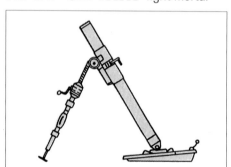

The first Soviet 82-mm mortar, the M-37 is of conventional but sturdy design. Although it has been in military service for 60 years, it can still be found in inventories all over the world.

DURING THE COLD WAR Soviet motor rifle battalions re-equipped with 120-mm mortars, but naval infantry and airborne forces retained the pre-war **M1937** or **M-37 82-mm** weapon. This was an upgrade of an earlier design, copied from contemporary German and American weapons, and had been the Red Army's main portable mortar of the war.

To the elite forces which have continued to use it, the M-37 had the advantage of being man-portable and, supplied to left-wing forces all over the world, it has been used in countless guerrilla campaigns since 1945. Although some users made modifications – the North Vietnamese created a delayed-action fuse for use against American forces – the ammunition has otherwise not changed since the 1930s.

Post-war versions incorporated extra features, including a light tripod and a safety device that prevented bombs being loaded one on top of another. The **M-41** was designed as a replacement, but ballistic performance was so poor that the older mortar was retained in service.

SPECIFICATION
Name: M-37
Calibre: 82-mm
Barrel length: 1220 mm
Weight: 56 kg
Weight of bomb: 3.05 kg
Types of bomb: HE, smoke, fragmentation
Rate of fire: 15-25 rpm
Minimum range: 100 m
Maximum range: 3000 m
Users: Russia, former Soviet republics, Albania, Bulgaria, China, Congo, Cuba, Czech republic, Egypt, Germany, Ghana, Indonesia, Iraq, North Korea, Slovakia, Syria, Vietnam, forces of former Yugoslav republics

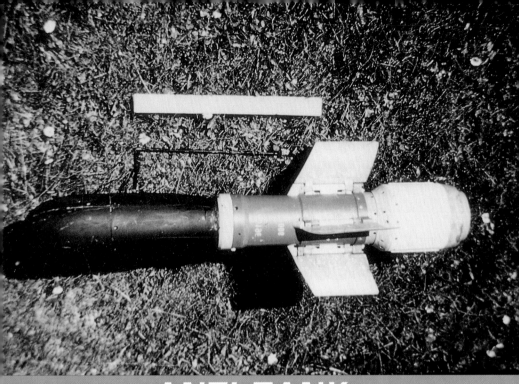

ANTI-TANK

MILAN infantry anti-tank missile

THE MAN-PORTABLE **MILAN** is the best of the second generation of wire-guided anti-tank missiles. It started life as far back as 1962, when Nord Aviation and Messerschmitt-Bölkow Blohm set up a joint study on the development of a light, man-portable missile of great accuracy and penetrating power, and since that time it has become one of the most successful weapons of its type ever developed.

MILAN stands for **Missile d'Infanterie Léger Anti-char**, or light infantry anti-tank missile. It is primarily designed to be used by infantry firing from a defensive position. Produced by the multinational Euromissile consortium, it is manufactured under licence in Britain. It has sold widely, with more than 250,000 being delivered to armies all over the world. The Soviet AT-4 'Spigot' is closely based on the same design.

Missiles come in factory-sealed tubes which are

MILAN is one of the world's most successful guided weapons. Easily handled by two men, it is far from lightweight in its effect – the latest version can destroy most modern tanks.

fitted to a re-usable firing post. On firing, a gas generator inside the tube blows the missile forwards and, after it has travelled a safe distance from the operator, the missile's own motor powers it on its 13-second flight to the target. France, Britain and Germany have given MILAN significant new capability by adopting the MIRA thermal imager, which can detect tank-sized targets at ranges of more than 3000 metres.

Like all guided weapons, MILAN is expensive. At £15,000 per missile, live firing leaves as big a hole in the budget as it does in the target. As a result, much training is conducted on simulators that accurately replicate the firing characteristics of the weapon.

The addition of a thermal sight gives MILAN-equipped infantrymen the ability to engage enemy tanks day or night, in all weathers.

SPECIFICATION

Name: Milan (Missile d'Infanterie Léger Anti-Char)
Type: wire-guided anti-armour missile
Guidance: SACLOS (Semi-Automatic Command to Line Of Sight) with infra-red tracking
Launcher length: 900 mm
Missile length: 769 mm
Launcher weight: 27.7 kg
Maximum velocity: 200 metres per second at 2000 m
Warhead weight: 2.98 kg
Warhead diameter: 115 mm
Warhead type: HEAT
Range: minimum 25 metres, maximum 2000 metres
Armour penetration: 1000 mm
Users: France, Germany, UK, and more than 30 other armed forces

HOT heavy anti-tank missile

HOT IS A HEAVY ANTI-TANK WEAPON, capable of being fired from a launcher but primarily intended for vehicle launch. A second-generation weapon developed jointly by the Franco-German Euromissile consortium, HOT is in service with some 15 different armies.

Iraq used HOT from vehicles and helicopters during the war with Iran, but were on the receiving end during the Gulf War. Syrian forces employed it during the 1980s in Lebanon, managing to make some kills of Israeli tanks including the heavily-armoured Merkava then being introduced to combat. It is suspected that the design of the Soviet AT-5 'Spandrel' was based on stolen HOT technology.

HOT can engage most types of main battle tank beyond the effective range of their main armament. Fitted to missile-firing tank destroyers of the

HOT is a much heavier weapon than MILAN, roughly equivalent to the American TOW, and has found its forte as a weapon for mounting on armoured vehicles or on tank-killing helicopters.

German army, it has proved highly effective, although reloading is obviously much slower than on the equivalent gun-armed Jagdpanzers.

Germany uses HOT to arm its Jagdpanzer Jaguar missile-armed tank destroyers.

SPECIFICATION

Name: HOT (Haut subsonique Optiquement téléguidé tiré d'un Tube)
Type: wire-guided anti-armour missile
Guidance: SACLOS (Semi-Automatic Command to Line Of Sight) with automatic infra-red tracking
Launcher length: 1300 mm
Missile length: 1275 mm
Launch weight: 23.5 kg
Maximum velocity: 250 metres per second
Warhead weight: 6 kg
Warhead diameter: 136 mm
Warhead type: HEAT
Effective range: minimum 75 metres, maximum 4000 metres
Armour penetration: 1300 mm
Users: France, Germany and more than 12 other armed forces

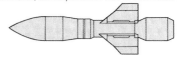

HOT's 6-kg shaped-charge warhead can penetrate more than 1.3 metres of armour plate.

FRANCE
ERYX short-range anti-tank missile

Eryx has been specifically designed to be fired from enclosed spaces, which was a very dangerous practice with earlier anti-armour weapons.

fire from within enclosed spaces since there is no backblast. The motor is at the front of the missile, exhausting through two vents at the centre of gravity. ERYX is wire-guided; the gunner keeps his sights on the target and the missile is automatically steered to ensure a hit. The powerful tandem charge warhead has the penetrating effect of a much heavier missile.

ERYX IS THE 'BIG GAME HUNTER'S' choice among modern man-portable anti-armour systems. Designed for short-range anti-armour engagements by forward-deployed infantry at ranges between 50 and 600 metres, its large-calibre shaped-charge warhead is intended to give it a better chance of killing a modern main battle tank from the front than is possible with other infantry anti-tank weapons.

The missile is blasted clear of the launch tube by a small charge, which is exhausted before the missile clears the muzzle. This makes Eryx safe to

SPECIFICATION
Name: ERYX
Type: short-range wire-guided anti-tank missile
Guidance: SACLOS (Semi-Automatic Command to Line Of Sight)
Launcher length: 925 mm
Launcher weight: 15.4 kg
Round weight: 12 kg
Maximum velocity: 300 metres per second
Effective range: 600 m
Warhead weight: 3.6 kg
Warhead diameter: 160 mm
Warhead type: HEAT
Armour penetration: 900 mm
Users: France

ISRAEL
82-mm B-300 light anti-armour rocket

Light and easy to operate, the B-300 lacks the ability to deal with really thick armour, but it works very well as a bunker-buster.

through (HEFT) round blows a hole in the target with a shaped charge, then catapults a secondary charge into the interior of the target before exploding.

The B-300 forms the basis for the McDonnell Douglas Shoulder-launched Multi-purpose Assault Weapon or SMAW, ordered in large numbers for the US armed forces. It is equipped with a spotting rifle and a new telescopic sight, and is primarily an anti-bunker weapon. SMAW rockets are fitted with a larger multi-purpose warhead, and the system in American use is much heavier than the original.

INSPIRED BY THE SOVIET-MADE RPG-7 and the French LRAC 89, the **B-300** light anti-armour weapon improves on both. With its small-diameter warhead it lacks the ability to penetrate the armour of modern main battle tanks, but against light armoured vehicles it is highly effective.

The B-300 consists of two parts: a re-usable sight and a gripstock connected to the muzzle, to which the rounds, packed in the disposable tubes that include the breech, are inserted before firing. It fires rocket-powered fin-stabilised rounds equipped with HEAT warheads. The high-explosive follow-

SPECIFICATION
Name: B-300
Type: unguided rocket-launcher
Launcher length: 1400 mm ready to fire
Launcher weight: 5.5 kg
Round weight: 4.5 kg
Maximum velocity: 270 metres per second
Effective range: 400 m
Warhead weight: 3.1 kg
Warhead diameter: 82 mm
Warhead type: HEAT, tandem charge HEAT, illuminating
Armour penetration: more than 400 mm
Users: Israel, United States

84-mm M2 Carl-Gustav recoilless anti-tank gun

THIS SWEDISH-DESIGNED recoilless rifle is one of the most widely used short-range anti-tank weapons in the world. The **M2 Carl Gustav** is an 84-mm weapon which was until recently the British Army's standard section medium anti-tank weapon. The M3 Carl Gustav is a lightweight version, which is used by American special forces.

Many armies prefer to keep an unguided anti-tank weapon with the fighting troops. Recoilless guns are cheaper, easier to use and maintain, and have a far higher rate of fire than missile systems like the American Dragon or rocket-propelled grenades like the Soviet RPG-7.

A well-trained two-man team can fire more than six rounds per minute from a Carl Gustav. The variety of 84-mm ammunition available meant that the gun is far more versatile than most missiles.

The Carl Gustav is aimed through a x2 telescope and usually fired from the shoulder or from a bipod. It can be fired by one man, but a two-man team of gunner and loader is more usual.

A wide range of ammunition has been manufactured for the Carl Gustav system, which makes the gun very effective as a bunker-buster and anti-personnel weapon as well as a tank destroyer.

The Carl Gustav's rifled barrel gives it the accuracy to hit bunkers at ranges of up to 500 metres.

SPECIFICATION
Name: M2/M3 Carl Gustav gun
Type: recoilless rifled anti-tank gun
Launcher length: 1130 mm ready to fire
Launcher weight: 14.2 kg
Round weight: 2.6 kg
Muzzle velocity: 310 metres per second
Effective range: moving targets 300 m; bunkers 500 m; exposed troops 1000 m; smoke 1300 m; illumination 2300 m
Warhead weight: 1.7 kg
Warhead diameter: 84 mm
Warhead type: HEAT; rocket-assisted HEAT; HE; dual-purpose HE/anti-armour; illuminating; smoke
Armour penetration: more than 400 mm
Users: several countries including Denmark, Sweden, United Kingdom, USA, and Venezuela

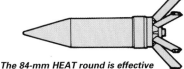

The 84-mm HEAT round is effective against most types of armour.

Bantam infantry anti-tank missile

Bantam was a very early example of a man-portable missile, which is still capable of dealing with light armoured vehicles.

manually guided to the target, the operator keeping track of the missile through a monocular sight as he flies it towards the target like a model aeroplane. Bright flares burn in its tail to help the operator see where it is going.

THE BOFORS **BANTAM** IS a first-generation man-portable anti-tank guided missile purchased by the armies of Switzerland and Sweden in the 1960s. One of the smallest and lightest of early ATGMs, the missile is supplied in a container with a 20-metre control cable that is connected to a control unit. Each unit can take up to three missiles, although by using distribution boxes this total can be increased to 18.

Unlike more modern weapons, the Bantam is

SPECIFICATION

Name: Bantam
Type: wire-guided anti-armour missile
Guidance: manual command
Launcher length: c. 1000 mm
Missile length: 848 mm
Launch weight: 7.6 kg
Maximum velocity: 85 metres per second
Warhead weight: 1.9 kg
Warhead diameter: 100 mm
Warhead type: hollow charge
Effective range: minimum 300 metres, maximum 2000 metres
Armour penetration: 500 mm
Users: Sweden, Switzerland

Bofors RBS-56 BILL top-attack anti-tank missile

BILL was the first infantry missile designed to engage a tank's vulnerable upper surfaces.

number were purchased by the US Army for evaluation as a replacement for the Dragon.

SPECIFICATION

Name: RBS-56 BILL
Type: wire-guided anti-armour missile
Guidance: SACLOS (Semi-Automatic Command to Line Of Sight)
Missile length: 900 mm
Launcher weight: 38 kg
Missile weight: 16 kg
Maximum velocity: 250 metres per second
Warhead diameter: 150 mm
Warhead type: downward-directed high-explosive shaped charge
Effective range: minimum 150 metres, maximum 2000 metres
Armour penetration: classified, but probably in excess of 1000 mm
Users: Sweden, Austria; under evaluation by several other armies

PROPERLY KNOWN AS THE **BOFORS RBS-56**, this revolutionary Swedish missile is more commonly known as **BILL**. The name comes from a somewhat laboured acronym meaning **'Bofors, Infantry, Light and Lethal'**. BILL is the first man-portable missile designed to attack the top of tanks where their armour is thinner.

BILL is programmed to fly exactly one metre above the sight line, which takes it across the top of the target tank. A proximity fuse automatically fires the angled warhead when it is within lethal range. The shaped charge shoots an explosive jet down through the thin roof of the tank, with devastating effect on the interior.

BILL is in use with the Swedish army and a

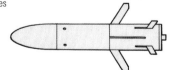

BILL's unique top-attack profile means that it can destroy any known main battle tank.

Swingfire heavy anti-tank missile

Swingfire's warhead can penetrate the thickest of tank armour (left). However, it is a large missile and a bit of a handful on the ground, so it is usually mounted on Striker armoured vehicles.

Swingfire can be operated by dismounted infantry, requiring a three-man team, and also in separated fire mode, controlled by an operator up to 100 metres from the launcher. In such a case, the missile is automatically gathered into the operator's line of sight, from where it is manually guided to the target. The current upgrade will convert this to fully automatic command to line of sight guidance.

SWINGFIRE IS THE BRITISH equivalent of TOW or HOT. It has a similar guidance system, allied to an even larger warhead capable of penetrating all current armour types. First entering service in 1969, Swingfire has had some reliability problems, but is currently being upgraded with new guidance and tracking systems.

Swingfire was intended to be used by mobile armoured troops, and as such is primarily a vehicle-mounted system, equipping the Striker armoured vehicles of the British and Belgian armies. A palletised version is built under licence in Egypt, which can be mounted on any vehicle or trainer of Land Rover size or larger.

SPECIFICATION
Name: Swingfire
Type: wire-guided anti-armour missile
Guidance: manual command to line of sight
Launcher length: 1100 mm
Missile length: 1060 mm
Launch weight: 27 kg
Warhead weight: 7 kg
Warhead diameter: c. 150 mm
Warhead type: hollow charge
Effective range: minimum 150 metres, maximum 4000 metres
Armour penetration: more than 1000 mm
Users: United Kingdom, Belgium, Egypt

LAW 80 light anti-tank weapon

Weighing in at 10 kg, the pre-packed and factory-sealed LAW 80 can be carried by a soldier in addition to his normal weapons load.

against modern MBTs. The LAW 80 projectile has a 94-mm diameter warhead which is capable of destroying most likely targets. Straightforward to operate and highly reliable, the LAW 80 is treated as a round of ammunition, needing little special treatment or preparation before firing. It has an integral five-round spotting rifle that fires tracer rounds, enabling the operator to correct his aim before letting go with the main round.

LAW 80 can also be used as part of an automatic off-route or remotely-fired weapon, when it is known as Addermine or Addermine Ajax.

LAW 80 IS A ONE-SHOT disposable rocket launcher adopted by the British Army during the late 1980s. It is one metre long and weighs 10 kilograms. These dimensions are dictated by the need for it to be small enough for a rifleman to carry one in addition to his kit, while at the same time being armed with a warhead large enough to threaten modern tanks.

The 1960s vintage American LAW, used by British soldiers in the Falklands to attack enemy bunkers, fires a 66-mm rocket that is ineffective

SPECIFICATION
Name: LAW 80 light anti-armour weapon
Type: one-shot short-range rocket-launcher
Launcher length: 1500 mm ready to fire
Launcher weight: 10 kg
Round weight: 4 kg
Effective range: 20 m-500 m
Warhead weight: c.2 kg
Warhead diameter: 94 mm
Warhead type: HEAT
Armour penetration: more than 700 mm
Users: British forces

USA

3.5-in M20 recoilless rocket-launcher

In service for nearly half a century, the M20 anti-tank rocket-launcher is long obsolete, but it can still be found with armies all over the world.

mechanism – magneto or two AA batteries in more modern versions – that launches fin-stabilised rockets at the modest velocity of 160 metres per second. The rocket warhead is a shaped charge with a steel ballistic head and a percussion fuse at the base of the warhead.

Very simple to use, the M20 is handicapped by its short range and limited armour penetration. Its performance is poor by comparison with modern HEAT rounds.

THE US 3.5-INCH **M20 ROCKET-LAUNCHER** was widely known as the 'super bazooka', as it replaced the 2.36-in Bazooka of World War II fame. Adopted after World War II by many NATO countries, it has been superseded in most major armies but remains in use elsewhere. Versions of the M20 were still being manufactured until recently in Austria and Spain.

Recoilless rocket-launchers are very simple weapons, little more than smoothbore tubes open at both ends, with some kind of electrical connection to ignite an anti-tank rocket. The M20 launcher is a two-piece aluminium tube with a firing

SPECIFICATION
Name: M20 rocket-launcher
Type: recoilless rocket-launcher
Launcher length: 1549 mm
Launcher weight: 5.5 kg
Round weight: 4.04 kg
Effective range: 110 m
Warhead weight: 0.87 kg
Warhead diameter: 89 mm
Warhead type: HEAT
Armour penetration: 250 mm
Users: obsolete in first-line armies, but can still be found in many African, Latin American and Asian countries

---

USA

106-mm M40 recoilless anti-tank gun

The M40 can be manhandled, but it is more often found on jeeps or in fixed defensive positions.

ready for the main round, greatly improving his chance of hitting the target.

Adopted by over 30 armies and still widely encountered today, Spain and Austria both manufacture very similar weapons, and it has been built under licence in Brazil, Israel and Japan.

ENTERING SERVICE IN THE 1950S, the **M40** 106-mm recoilless rifle is one of the most successful non-Soviet weapons of its type. Actually 105 mm in calibre, it is a development of the earlier M27 weapon, and to avoid supply confusion ammunition for the new weapon was redesignated.

The 'wheelbarrow'-like tripod mounting can be manoeuvred on the ground or clamped to a vehicle – typically a jeep. The HEAT round is supplemented by a HEP (High-Explosive Plastic) round, similar to the British HESH ammunition, plus a specialised anti-personnel round which was widely used in Vietnam. The M40 was the first medium anti-tank weapon to be fitted with a spotting rifle. By firing a few tracer rounds, the operator can adjust his aim

SPECIFICATION
Name: M40
Type: recoilless rifled anti-tank gun
Launcher length: 3404 mm
Launcher weight: 209.5 kg
Round weight: 16.9-18.25 kg
Effective range: 1100 m;
Warhead weight: 8 kg
Warhead diameter: 105 mm
Warhead type: HEAT; HEP, anti-personnel
Armour penetration: more than 400 mm
Users: USA (reserve); supplied to more than 30 countries since the 1950s and can be encountered all over the world

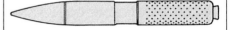

Although large, the 105-mm round lacks the armour penetration of modern missiles.

M47 Dragon infantry anti-tank missile

THE **M47 DRAGON** HAS BEEN the US Army's medium infantry anti-tank weapon since the 1970s. Older and less capable than systems like MILAN, its maximum range of only 1000 metres is now considered inadequate, and its unusual propulsion and control system offers little advantage over more conventional designs.

Dragon has 60 side-thrust rocket motors on its outer surface, and rolls as it flies. Each rocket fires as it reaches bottom centre, both giving the missile lift and propelling the missile forwards. The gunner merely has to keep the sight on target and the missile will be guided automatically. Steering signals are sent down wires unreeling behind the missile, and pairs of rockets fire to provide course correction.

The USA's Dragon infantry anti-tank missile lives up to its name when being fired – but the spectacular backblast is a real giveaway in tactical situations.

The current service version is the **M47 Dragon II**, which substantially increases its penetration although the maximum range remains at 1000 metres. The latest **Dragon III** has a tandem war-head and an increased range of 1500 metres.

SPECIFICATION

Name: M47 Dragon
Type: wire-guided anti-armour missile
Guidance: SACLOS (Semi-Automatic Command to Line Of Sight) with infra-red tracking
Launcher length: 1154 mm
Missile length: 774 mm
Launcher weight: 14 kg
Maximum velocity: 100 metres per second
Warhead weight: 2.45 kg
Warhead type: HEAT
Effective range: 75-1000 metres
Armour penetration: 500 mm
Users: more than 15 countries including USA, Israel, Jordan, Morocco, Netherlands, Saudi Arabia, Spain, Switzerland, Thailand and former Yugoslavian states

The Dragon is steered automatically – all the gunner has to do is to keep the target centred in the sight while a micro-computer controls the missile.

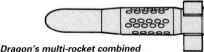

Dragon's multi-rocket combined propulsion/sustainer system is unique.

BGM-71 TOW heavy anti-tank missile

OFFICIALLY KNOWN TO THE US ARMY as the **BGM-71**, the missile is more commonly known as **TOW**, standing for **Tube-launched, Optically sighted, Wire-guided**. It made its combat debut to stunning effect in Vietnam in 1972 and was to prove equally successful during the 1973 Arab-Israeli war, when large shipments were rushed to Israel by US military aircraft. It is the most widely used of all heavy anti-tank missiles, in service worldwide

Although it can be used from a tripod by infantry

A TOW 2 missile is puffed clear of its launch tube, control fins and nose probe flicking out in the instant before the main propulsion motor ignites.

on foot, TOW's large size and heavy weight make it more suitable as part of a fixed defensive line or on vehicle or helicopter mountings.

The basic missile consists of a shaped-charge warhead with a launch motor and a flight motor. Thermal and xenon beacons identify the missile in flight and help the operator steer it onto the target. The US Army deployed a more capable version, **Improved TOW**, but now uses **TOW 2**, which has a bigger warhead with substantially better armour-piercing characteristics. **TOW 2A** adds a second tandem charge to defeat reactive armour, while **TOW 2B** is designed for top attack.

TOW 2's nose probe detonates the main warhead just before it hits the target. This gives the molten jet from the shaped charge explosive more room to form an efficient armour-penetrating form.

SPECIFICATION

Name: BGM-71D TOW 2
Type: wire-guided anti-armour missile
Guidance: SACLOS (Semi-Automatic Command to Line Of Sight) with infra-red tracking
Launcher length: 2210 mm
Missile length: 1174 mm
Launcher weight: 93 kg
Maximum velocity: 200 metres per second
Warhead weight: 10 kg
Warhead diameter: 152 mm
Warhead type: HEAT
Effective range: 65–3750 metres
Armour penetration: more than 1000 mm
Users: USA and more than 40 other armies, including those of most NATO countries

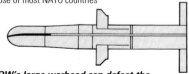

TOW's large warhead can defeat the armour of any known tank.

RPG-7 rocket-propelled grenade-launcher

The RPG-7 has seen extensive combat in the Middle East since its introduction in 1962.

RPG-7s have been used more often against Communist forces – in Afghanistan, Nicaragua and Angola – than by them.

THE **RPG-7** IS ONE OF THE MOST widely used anti-armour weapons in the world. It is a simple design, derived from the wartime German Panzerfaust. Firing a muzzle-loaded 85-mm rocket propelled anti-tank grenade with a shaped-charge warhead from a 40-mm launch tube, the RPG-7 was issued in huge numbers to the old Soviet army. It was also exported all over the world, and will be seen in trouble spots around the world for many years to come. It has been produced in the Soviet Union, China, and a number of licensed and unlicensed Third World nations. Both sides in the Iran-Iraq war made extensive use of RPG-7s. Ironically,

SPECIFICATION
Name: Reaktivniy Protivotankoviy Granatomet-7
Type: rocket-propelled grenade launcher
Launcher length: 950 mm
Launcher weight: 8.6 kg
Round weight: 2 kg
Maximum velocity: 120 metres per second
Effective range: 300 m
Warhead diameter: 85 mm
Warhead type: HEAT
Armour penetration: 300 mm
Users: former Soviet and Warsaw pact armies; in widespread use in Africa, Asia and the Middle East

RPG-7s were used in Afghanistan to fire high-explosive anti-personnel rounds.

Soviet Recoilless rifles recoilless anti-tank gun

Palestinian guerrillas load a Chinese copy of the B-10 at the height of the Lebanese conflict. The 82-mm gun had a maximum range of around 4000 metres when firing HE rounds, but accuracy was poor.

Introduced in 1969, the **SPG-9** is a lightweight recoilless anti-tank gun which replaced the older weapons in Soviet and Warsaw Pact use. Operated by a two-man crew, and capable of being carried by a four-man team, its 73-mm fin-stabilised rounds are rocket-assisted and have a muzzle velocity of over 700 metres per second. The SPG-9 is mounted on a light tripod and is normally carried inside a vehicle, until deployment is required. The anti-tank platoon of each Soviet Motor Rifle battalion was equipped with two SPG-9s.

THE STANDARD POST-WAR Soviet recoilless anti-tank weapons were the **82-mm B-10** and the **107-mm B-11** guns. Effective at up to 400 metres, they could penetrate between 200 and 400 mm of armour. Although designed primarily as anti-armour weapons, they could also fire high-explosive fragmentation rounds, and were often employed as man-portable artillery. Widely used in the Middle East and in Southeast Asia, the B-10 was a favoured weapon of the Viet Cong during the Vietnam War.

SPECIFICATION
Name: SPG-9
Type: recoilless anti-tank gun
Launcher length: 2110 mm
Launcher weight: 47.5 kg
Round weight: 1.3 kg
Maximum velocity: 700 metres per second
Effective range: 1300 m
Warhead diameter: 73 mm
Warhead type: HEAT, HE, rocket-assisted
Armour penetration: 400 mm
Users: former Soviet republics, Bulgaria, Hungary, Poland

AT-3 'Sagger' infantry anti-tank missile

Left: In infantry operation a three-man 'Sagger' team can set up a four-missile position within 15 minutes. Missiles can be deployed up to 15 metres from the central sight and control unit.

Below: 'Sagger' is carried into action in two parts, with warhead and motor joined before firing. The launch rail is attached to the motor section, and is mounted on the lid of the glass-reinforced plastic carrying case, which is used as a launch platform.

THE SOVIET-DESIGNED wire-guided anti-tank missile known to its Russian users as **9K11/9M14 Malyutka** is better known around the world by the NATO designation **AT-3 'Sagger'**. It was one of the first truly effective man-portable guided missiles, with which the Egyptian infantry inflicted a surprise defeat on Israeli armour in the first days of the 1973 Arab-Israeli war.

Early 'Saggers' were manually controlled, requiring a skilled operator and difficult to use when under fire. The interim **'Sagger B'** had the same guidance system but was fitted with a more efficient rocket motor which gave a 25 per cent increase in speed. During the 1970s the Soviets introduced a version with semi-automatic guidance, which became known to NATO as **'Sagger C'**. Both of the later types armed Mil-8 'Hip' and early Mil-24 'Hind' helicopters, as well as BRDM scout cars and BMP infantry fighting vehicles.

In combat, the operator collects the missile into his field of view on launch. At engagement ranges below 1000 metres, the 'Sagger' operator guides the missile by eye. At longer ranges the operator uses the x10 magnification optical sight to locate the missile and steer it into the target, helped by high-visibility flares in the tail.

In spite of the fact that its warhead cannot deal with the advanced armour of the latest main battle tanks, 'Sagger' remains in worldwide service as an infantry, vehicle and helicopter weapon with ex-Soviet and Warsaw Pact armies as well as in former Soviet client states.

SPECIFICATION
Name: 9K11/9M14 Malyutka (AT-3 'Sagger')
Type: wire-guided anti-armour missile
Guidance: manual/SACLOS (Semi-Automatic Command to Line Of Sight) with optical tracking
Missile length: 880 mm
Launch weight: 11.3 kg
Maximum velocity: 200 metres per second
Warhead diameter: 120 mm
Warhead type: HEAT
Effective range: minimum 300 metres, maximum 3000 metres
Armour penetration: more than 400 mm
Users: former Soviet and Warsaw Pact, Cuba, India, North Korea, and more than 12 African and Middle Eastern countries

USSR/RUSSIA

RPG-18 light anti-tank weapon

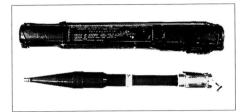

The RPG-18 is a simple one-shot weapon which is not much use against tanks, but well suited to engaging light armour or field fortifications.

An improved version of the light anti-armour weapon was fielded in the last days of the Afghanistan conflict. Given the NATO designation **RPG-22**, this is thought to be of similar design but with an 80-mm calibre, offering considerably more armour penetration.

THE **RPG-18** IS THE SOVIET equivalent of the American M72 LAW which has been in service since the 1960s. It follows the same format, being a one-shot disposable weapon in an extendable tube with pop-up sights and cartoon instructions painted on the side. It fires a 64-mm calibre shaped charge, compared with the 66-mm warhead of the old US weapon. It does not have sufficient penetration to knock out the latest generation of tanks, but is effective enough as a bunker-buster or against armoured personnel carriers and light vehicles. Several Warsaw Pact countries had begun to manufacture the RPG-18 by the time the alliance disintegrated at the end of the 1980s.

SPECIFICATION

Name: Reaktivniy Protivotankoviy Granatomet-18
Type: lightweight anti-armour rocket launcher
Launcher length: 705 mm
Launcher weight: 2.7 kg
Round weight: 1.4 kg
Maximum velocity: 115 metres per second
Effective range: 300 m
Warhead diameter: 64 mm
Warhead type: HEAT
Armour penetration: 375 mm
Users: Russia, former Soviet republics, some ex-Warsaw Pact countries

---

USSR/RUSSIA

AT-4 'Spigot' infantry anti-tank missile

'Spigot' is taken into action in the same way as the preceding 'Sagger'. Four missiles are usually carried by two members of the three-man fire team, with the third carrying the firing post and sight.

AT-7 'Saxhorn'. It is a simpler design with better electronics, intended for shorter-range engagements at up to 1000 metres. Normally fired like the AT-4 from a mount, at very short range it can also be fired from the shoulder.

DURING THE 1980s the Soviets introduced a series of new and advanced anti-tank guided weapons, of which the man-portable or vehicle-mounted **9K111/9M111 Fagot** received the NATO designation **AT-4 'Spigot'**

It is very similar to but a little smaller than MILAN – according to US sources the design was stolen from Euromissile – and is operated in the same fashion. 'Spigot' was also supplied to Polish, Czech and the former East German armies. The launcher can also fire the **9P/148/9M113 Konkurs**, an enlarged missile designated **AT-5 'Spandrel'** in the West. Based on the 'Spigot', this has double the range and is normally mounted on vehicles or helicopters.

The AT-4 represents a major advance over the old manual-command weapons like 'Sagger', but it is known to have been supplemented in the late 1980s by a smaller and lighter weapon. The **9K115/9M115 Metis** has the NATO designation

SPECIFICATION

Name: 9K111/9M111 Fagot (AT-4 'Spigot')
Type: wire-guided anti-armour missile
Guidance: SACLOS (Semi-Automatic Command to Line Of Sight) with optical or infra-red tracking
Launcher length: 1200 mm
Missile length: c. 1000 mm
Missile weight: .12 kg
Maximum velocity: 200 metres per second
Warhead weight: c. 3 kg
Warhead type: HEAT
Effective range: 500-2500 m
Armour penetration: more than 500 mm
Users: Russia, former Soviet republics and some ex-Warsaw Pact nations

'Spigot' bears a striking resemblance to the slightly larger Euromissile MILAN.

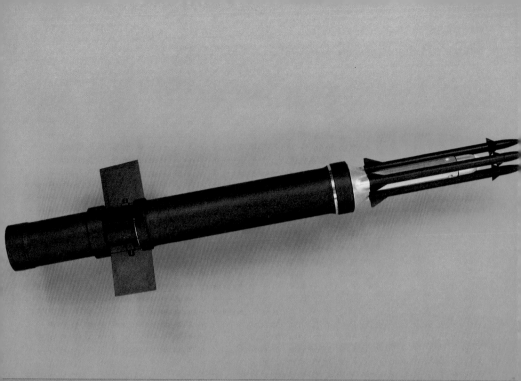

SURFACE-TO-AIR MISSILES

FRANCE
SATCP Mistral man-portable surface-to-air missile

Mistral's most easily recognisable feature is the pyramid-shaped seeker. Highly sensitive, it can lock on to a non-afterburning jet at 6000 metres and a helicopter at 4000 metres.

before the main motor ignites. Mistral has a cooled passive infra-red seeker derived from the MATRA Magic air-to-air missile, designed to home in on the target aircraft's exhaust plume.

DEVELOPED FOR THE FRENCH armed forces, the **SATCP (Sol-Air Très Courte Portée, or surface-to-air very short range) Mistral** entered service in the late 1980s. The missile used by the infantry is post-mounted, and the whole system can be broken down into two 20-kg loads. It is also available in vehicle-, ship- and air-launched versions.

The firing post mounts a x3 telescope, which is used to identify targets detected by eye or by third-party sources such as observers or a radar net. On firing, the missile is blown clear of the launch tube

> **SPECIFICATION**
> **Name: Mistrale**
> **Type:** man-portable surface-to-air missile
> **Guidance:** passive infra-red heat-seeking
> **Missile length:** 1.8 m
> **Missile weight:** 17.0 kg
> **Fire unit weight:** 20 kg
> **Maximum velocity:** Mach 2.6
> **Effective range:** 500 m minimum, 6000 m maximum
> **Warhead weight:** 3.0 kg
> **Warhead type:** HE with laser proximity fuse
> **Users:** France, Abu Dhabi, Belgium, Cyprus, Finland, Gabon, Italy, Saudi Arabia, Spain
>
>
>
> *Mistral can be used without modification in air-to-air and naval applications.*

SWEDEN
RBS 70 man-portable surface-to-air missile

Entering service in the late 1970s, the laser-beam-riding RBS 70 is available in vehicle- and ship-launched versions. It can be used independently, but to make the system more effective it can also accept target data from air defence radar systems.

optics. The pre-fragmented warhead contains a large number of heavy metal balls and is detonated either by a direct hit or by means of a proximity fuse.

> *The RBS 70 was one of the first beam-riding man-portable missiles.*
>
>

THE **RBS 70** SAM SYSTEM consists of three main components, namely the stand incorporating gunner's seat, laser sight with aiming telescope, and missile in its launch tube, each of which can be transported by one man. For night operations the sight can be fitted with an infra-red scanning unit. The complete system can be assembled in about 30 seconds.

The sight generates a modulated laser beam which coincides with the line of sight. On being launched the missile crosses the guidance beam, which it follows until it hits the target. All the operator has to do is to keep the sight on the target, using a thumb lever to control the gyro-stabilised

SPECIFICATION
Name: RBS 70
Type: man-portable surface-to-air missile
Guidance: laser beam riding
Missile length: 1.32 m
Missile weight: 24 kg including sealed container
Fire unit weight: 56 kg
Maximum velocity: supersonic
Effective range: 5000 m horizontal, 3000 m vertical
Warhead weight: 1.1 kg
Warhead type: HE fragmentation with active optical fuse
Users: Sweden, Argentina, Bahrain, Iran, Ireland, Indonesia, Norway, Pakistan, Singapore, Tunisia, UAE, Venezuela

Javelin shoulder-launched surface-to-air-missile

THE **JAVELIN** IS A FOLLOW-ON design to the highly successful Blowpipe missile used in more than a dozen countries. Basically similar to the earlier missile, Javelin has a more powerful warhead and an updated guidance system. Blowpipe was command-guided, and had to be flown by the operator using a thumb-operated joystick. This required a considerable degree of skill on the part of the firer.

Javelin is a semi-automatic command to line of

Javelin was designed to engage low-flying aircraft and helicopters. It is supersonic, and can reach most combat aircraft flying at battlefield speeds. Because it is command-guided it can be used to attack aircraft head-on, where most heat-seeking missiles need to home in from the tail.

sight weapon, which is automatically directed by radio command to where the monocular optical sight or the zoom television camera in the sight unit is pointing. To ensure a hit the operator simply has to maintain his sights on the target. Because it does not employ infra-red homing, Javelin is immune to enemy countermeasures such as decoy flares.

The sighting unit clips on to the missile canister. It takes less than five seconds to be prepared for combat action.

The Javelin missile has a longer range than the similar Blowpipe.

SPECIFICATION
Name: Javelin
Type: shoulder-launched surface-to-air missile
Missile length: 1.35 m
Missile weight: 15.4 kg
Aiming unit weight: 8.9 kg
Maximum velocity: supersonic
Effective range: minimum 300 m; 5500 m maximum
Guidance: semi-automatic command to line of sight
Warhead weight: 3.0 kg
Warhead type: HE pre-fragmented with laser proximity fuse
Users: United Kingdom, Botswana, Dubai, Jordan, Malaysia, Oman, South Korea

Starstreak shoulder-launched surface-to-air missile

IN THE EARLY 1980S the British Army issued a requirement for a battlefield air defence system, which called for a high-velocity missile with a high kill probability. Shorts' **Starstreak Close Air Defence Weapon System**, which entered service in the early 1990s, is twice as fast as rival missiles, and its unique submunition warhead is unmatched anywhere in the world.

The Starstreak's operator acquires the target in his monocular sight. Firing launches the missile and generates a laser beam along which the missile will ride. All the operator has to do is keep the target centred in his sight. Since the missile does not require heat-seeking, it can engage targets from all aspects.

The first-stage motor ejects the missile from its tube, with the main motor cutting in once the missile is safely clear of the operator. This acceler-

Starstreak is classed as a high-velocity missile. Its extremely high speed and seven-kilometre range enable the advanced weapon system to engage any aircraft currently flying.

ates Starstreak to hypersonic speeds. Once the motor burns out, the triple darts separate, their individual warheads arm, and they use their own guidance systems to take up a triangular formation around the laser beam. The heavy-metal darts have both kinetic energy and explosive effect, being designed to penetrate their target before exploding inside, for maximum effect.

Starstreak's unique triple-dart warhead, each submunition guiding individually, gives it considerably more killing power than a normal missile.

Starstreak's sight generates a laser beam which the missile follows automatically. It has a very accurate hit probability, estimated at 96 per cent.

SPECIFICATION

Name: Starstreak
Type: high-velocity shoulder-launched surface-to-air missile
Guidance: laser beam riding
Missile length: 1.397 m
System weight: not revealed, but probably between 20 and 25 kg
Maximum velocity: (estimated) Mach 4
Effective range: 300 m minimum, 7000 m maximum
Warhead weight: classified
Warhead type: triple kinetic/high explosive submunitions with delayed-action contact fuses
User: United Kingdom

FIM-92 Stinger shoulder-launched surface-to-air missile

THE **STINGER** MAN-PORTABLE surface-to-air missile system, officially designated **FIM-92**, was developed to intercept and destroy both hovering helicopters and high-speed manoeuvring targets. It became operational with the US Army in 1981, replacing the much less capable Redeye which had been in service since 1967.

Current Stingers include the **FIM-92B Stinger POST** and the **FIM-92C Stinger RMP**. These have advanced electro-optical seekers sensitive to both infra-red and ultra-violet, which can more effectively discriminate between targets and their background; this is of particular use when engaging aircraft at very low level.

The operator visually acquires the target and aligns this with the open sight on the launcher. He then uses his belt-mounted IFF system, which is

The Stinger is very simple to operate. Partially depressing the trigger activates the missile seeker head. This takes about five seconds to acquire the target. The sight then emits a growl, and the gunner launches by pulling the trigger all the way.

claimed to be the smallest of its type in the world to identify the aircraft positively. If it is confirmed as hostile he launches the missile, which homes in on the enemy aircraft without any further action by the operator. The gripstock is then detached from the empty launcher, which is discarded to permit a fresh launcher/missile to be attached.

SPECIFICATION

Name: FIM-92 Stinger

Type: shoulder-launched surface-to-air missile
Guidance: passive infra-red or IR/ultra-violet homing
Missile length: 1.52 m
Missile weight: 10.1 kg
Launcher weight: 5.6 kg
Maximum velocity: Mach 2.2
Effective range: 200 m minimum, 4500 m maximum
Warhead weight: 3.0 kg
Warhead type: HE fragmentation with contact fuse
Users: USA and more than 20 other countries, including Bahrain, Denmark, Germany, Greece, South Korea, Pakistan, Saudi Arabia and Switzerland

The basic Stinger missile has a hemispherical nose, transparent to infra-red radiation.

Re-usable components include grip stock, battery and battery coolant unit, and belt-mounted IFF.

SA-7 'Grail' shoulder-launched surface-to-air missile

Although fairly primitive by modern standards, the SA-7 'Grail' is relatively easy to use. It can be found with armies and guerrilla groups all over Africa, Asia and Latin America.

supersonic speed and the sustainer takes over. The infra-red seeker homes onto the exhaust of the aircraft or helicopter. The warhead is small, able to damage a target but less likely to destroy it.

MOST COMMONLY KNOWN by its NATO name, **SA-7 'Grail'**, the Russian **9M32 Strela** (Arrow) is one of the most widely-used missiles in the world. First seeing combat in the 1967 Middle East war, it consists of the missile in its launcher, a thermal battery and a reusable gripstock. The missile has an infra-red seeker head, two canard fins at the front and four spring-loaded stabilising tailfins.

When the seeker head has picked up sufficient infra-red radiation from the target, an audible warning is given and a light comes on. The trigger is then pulled right back and the missile is ejected by a launch motor. Once safely clear of the gunner a rocket booster then accelerates the missile to

SPECIFICATION
Name: 9M32 Strela 2 (SA-7 'Grail')
Type: shoulder-launched surface-to-air missile
Guidance: passive infra-red homing
Missile length: 1.34 m
Missile weight: 9.2 kg
Launcher weight: 4.17 kg
Maximum velocity: over Mach 1 (385 metres per second)
Effective range: 800 m minimum, 3700 m maximum
Warhead weight: 1.1 kg
Warhead type: HE frag with contact and graze fuse
Users: in service with more than 60 armies and more than 30 terrorist and guerrilla groups

The 'Grail' was one of the first true man-portable surface-to-air missiles.

SA-14 'Gremlin' shoulder-launched surface-to-air missile

First seen in action in Angola, the SA-16 is much more capable than the preceding SA-7.

and **SA-18 'Grouse'** respectively. They follow the same basic layout as the SA-7/SA-14 family, but with a new shoulder mount and a modified trigger and sight. The SA-16 has a small drag-reducing cone mounted a few centimetres ahead of the infra-red dome, while the SA-18 has a protruding spike.

KNOWN IN SOVIET AND RUSSIAN service as the **Strela 3**, the **SA-14 'Gremlin'** is a considerably updated development of the SA-7. Entering service in the late 1970s, it incorporates a more advanced seeker head able to keep lock on targets manoeuvring at up to 8*g*. It is also less vulnerable to decoys and capable of all-aspect engagements. It has a much more powerful motor, giving double the speed and improved range.

Since the early 1980s the SA-14 has been joined by two similar missiles, reportedly much more accurate. The **9M313 Igla 1** (Needle) and the **9M39 Igla** were given the NATO designations **SA-16 'Gimlet'**.

SPECIFICATION
Name: Strela 3 (SA-14 'Gremlin')
Type: shoulder-launched surface-to-air missile
Missile length: 1.4 m
Missile weight: 9.9 kg
Launcher weight: 6.1 kg
Maximum velocity: Mach 1.6
Effective range: 600 m minimum, 6000 m maximum
Guidance: passive infra-red homing
Warhead weight: 2.0 kg
Warhead type: HE fragmentation with contact and graze fuse
Users: in service with more than 20 ex-Soviet, Warsaw Pact and former Soviet client states

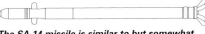

The SA-14 missile is similar to but somewhat heavier than the original SA-7 'Grail'.

Index